# Christians on the Right

# CHRISTIANS ON THE RIGHT

## The Moral Majority in Perspective

## JOHN L. KATER, Jr.

THE SEABURY PRESS · NEW YORK

1982
The Seabury Press
815 Second Avenue   New York, N.Y.   10017

**Library of Congress Cataloging in Publication Data**

Kater, John.
   Christians on the right.

   1. Christianity and politics.   2. Evangelicalism—
United States—History—20th century.   3. Conservatism—
United States—History—20th century.   4. United States—
Church history—20th century.   5. United States—Politics
and government—1977–1981.   6. United States—Politics and
government—1981–     .   I. Title.
BR115.P7K26      261.7        81-23334
ISBN 0-8164-2379-2                AACR2

pd
2-28-83

*To my parents*
who taught me that it is more important
to be moral than to be in the majority

## ACKNOWLEDGMENTS

This book could not have been written without the active help of many people, to whom I wish to express my gratitude.

The people of Christ Church, Poughkeepsie, New York, generously permitted me an extended absence from the parish to make possible my research and writing. More than they will ever know, they have also nurtured the faith and helped me formulate the perspective from which this book was written.

Sarah Southgate Gordon served as research assistant for the historical portions of the book, and did so with diligence, skill, and a creative and critical eye.

The Reverend David W. Perry, the Episcopal Church's Staff Officer for Adult Education, and the Reverend John M. Palmer III, Education Officer at Trinity Church, New York City, read the manuscript in its entirety and made many helpful suggestions in the course of its revision. John Ratti of Seabury Press served as editor with sensitivity and grace.

I am grateful to Michael Perry, Beth Rabenda, and Ame Weitzner for their assistance in the preparation of the manuscript.

Probably none of those to whom I am indebted would wish to endorse everything to be found in this book. However, I hope that they would be willing to accept my thanks for serving as guides to this pilgrim on his way.

# Contents

# Foreword

In the first two chapters of this book, the Christian Right is described as a contemporary religious phenomenon, on the right wing of the American political spectrum, couching its assumptions in traditional Christian language and imagery but with important political implications. Moreover, as a coherent unity, with its own values, norms, and mores, the Christian Right can lay claim to being a complete culture. Its adherents believe they are faithful guardians of the authentic culture of America's beginnings. It is true that they affirm some of the venerable theological girding on which America was founded. Nevertheless, they are in fact the heirs of a cultural perspective which emerged in opposition to the perceived holders of power: an Eastern, educated, affluent elite.

The sharp division between those with access to wealth, education, and power and those who saw themselves excluded soon developed into a continuing populist tradition, arrayed against those in power and buttressing its aims with appeals to popular religion and faithfulness to America's past. This tradition has been a perennial component of American political life, and survives into the present to inform the ambitions of the New Right. The religious foundations of that position remain largely unaltered. However, during populism's lifetime there have been revolutionary strides in secular learning, particularly with regard to the natural sciences. These developments clash directly with the religious perspective of the Right, which grew out of the fundamentalist Christianity of rural and small-town America. But the truth is that the Christian Right is not really interested in secular learning, and distrusts appeals to reason. Its authority rests instead on a particular style of theology. Any attempt to comprehend the movement without reference to its theological perspective is bound to fail.

In subsequent chapters, some of the basic articles of faith which Christians on the Right believe will be examined from the perspective of a critical theology based on the Incarnation. The purpose will be to form some judgment about how faithfully the New Right mirrors the affirmations of traditional Christian belief. It will also be important to note how those articles of faith function for their adherents in the Christian Right. This analysis will, I believe, demonstrate that the New Right's theology is in fact an ideological justification of already formed beliefs about the world and about Christians in the world.

The New Right's ideology of America would, if it came to dominate our culture, have significant and negative consequences which could be global in their effect. Like all ideology, its understanding of America claims to be built on certain fundamental principles which are objectively true. But, as I hope to demonstrate, its vision of America does not rest on the principles it claims to affirm. To the contrary, the fundamental Christian theological principles against which any society must be judged are drastically shortchanged by the New Right's vision of America. It is for that reason that its political vision must be resisted by those *whose faith may well rest on the same principles which the New Right claims to support.*

However, any examination of the movement which does not attempt to understand its appeal for countless numbers of Christian people would be incomplete. Christians who are critical of the Right can still respect the deep longings which form the experience behind its faith. The world we live in may not be as the New Right paints it for us, but we can nevertheless understand where its image came from, the hopes and fears which gave it birth. If the churches of the mainstream intend to take their mission seriously, those yearnings must be identified and addressed, without smugness and without patronizing. Furthermore, a genuinely critical look at the Christian Right cannot overlook the word of judgment on our churches from those who feel as genuinely excluded from our number as they find themselves alienated from other institutions which they identify with power and prestige.

I have no doubt that the posture of my own church is just as much in need of critical study as that of our neighbors to the right. (How often, for example, does the search for cultural "relevance," which we justify on "evangelical" grounds, mask a wish to justify a more sophisticated, more brilliant, more fashionable image of America? The temptation to ideology is not found exclusively on the Right.)

It is my hope that as Christians in the mainstream understand more fully the dreams and visions of the New Right, we will be challenged to put into practice more fully the values which they and we claim together. Whatever our place in the spectrum, nothing would serve us all better than a vision of America which took seriously the values we preach with such facility, and a church which mirrored in its life the love and justice against which every people must be judged.

# Turning America Around

> "As a pastor and as a parent I am calling my fellow American citizens to unite in a moral crusade for righteousness in our generation. . . . I am convinced that God is calling millions of Americans in the so-often silent majority to join in the moral-majority crusade to turn America around in our lifetime." [1]

That challenge from the Reverend Jerry Falwell, Baptist pastor, television preacher, and organizer of "Moral Majority, Inc." spells out the intentions of a religious movement which has swept into American political and religious consciousness with new fervor and undetermined influence. Its roots are as old as the nation itself. It is a challenge which affirms a way of living and believing derived from the American past, yet seeks to alter drastically the shape of our future. It speaks in the language of the Bible and traditional Christianity, but judges harshly many of the current concerns and choices of the churches. It is a movement capable of generating enormous passion: it calls forth deep loyalty, sacrificial giving, and uncritical acceptance from supporters, and contempt, anxiety, and hatred on the part of its opponents.

Furthermore, the movement represented by Falwell and others with similar views has announced its intention to make itself felt in the corridors of power, including the highest political offices of the land. Because it has strong opinions about politics and economics, its setting is the public arena where national decisions are made. It is entirely possible that the movement represented by the Moral Majority played a significant role in recent elections; it hopes and expects to be far more powerful in the electoral politics of the future.

Were these Christians of the New Right simply concerned about private belief and religious practice, their impact would be confined to individuals and perhaps churches. But although the movement does indeed make clear assumptions about the individual and the way faith operates in the private dimension of human experience, it also endorses and promotes a public vision of American society which it intends to call into being (or re-create). Its content is political, social, and economic, and it conceives of its vision as the *only* God-given option for American survival. Hence it battles with unflagging zeal for those aspects of its vision which will create or re-create an American society organized around the values it holds dear.

Those values are by definition *absolutes,* and are phrased in ways that draw inescapable—and unarguable—consequences. Many are well known; they include a strong military posture towards those who are understood to be inimical to American global interests; a religious understanding of American identity, expressed by public prayer in settings such as schoolrooms; an approach to education which defines its purpose as the inculcation of values assumed to be Christian; and a view of family life which precludes notions of equality between the sexes and which seeks to deal with perceived challenges to family integrity by legislation and prohibition.

The leaders of the movement approach the task of reshaping America with substantial resources and millions of supporters at their disposal. They are engaging the battle on many fronts: through the media, creation of alternative institutions such as schools and colleges, economic boycott of those opposed to their point of view, legal action, and, of course, at the ballot box. While estimates of their strength vary, it is plain that the religious New Right has already played a significant role in changing the complex mosaic of American social and political life. It is for these reasons that Falwell's challenge deserves to be taken seriously.

Perhaps Christians most of all ought to notice and respond to that challenge. At a time when many of the traditional denominations are experiencing a leveling off or even a decline in membership, Falwell's independent Baptist Church in Lynchburg, Virginia, claims a quarter of that city's population as members. When many church institutions are struggling for economic survival, some of the "stars" of the Christian Right can raise a million dollars *weekly*. After a century of wrestling with the implications for faith of scientific discoveries, critical study of the scriptures, and struggling through the social movements of recent times, many Christians whose allegiance has belonged to the traditional churches are intrigued by the New Right. They may wonder if these innovators, or reformers, are not closer to the ideals of biblical Christianity than the "mainline" denominations. Worried about the erosion of once-universal beliefs, they may long for the clarity and certainty of "old-time" religion. The New Right seems to offer authenticity, simplicity, and enthusiasm. Its advocates are usually attractive and preach a soothing message, but also hold out an appealing challenge to take control of the course of one's life.

Even if they are not attracted to the Moral Majority's vision of America, many Christians are concerned about the implications of ethical relativism. They wish they knew better what to teach their children about being moral. They long for a way out of the complexities in which so many contemporary problems seem ensnared: The more we know about world hunger or the population explosion, the more difficult it seems to know what to do. Simplicity is as attractive to church people as anyone else; so are ethical clarity and authoritative preaching.

Furthermore, most Christians educated in the main-line churches may well lack, or feel they lack, the tools they need to analyze critically the perspective of the religious New Right. They may wish they knew the Bible better, but they are rarely equipped to argue with the movement on its own terms. Non-fundamentalists seldom have sufficient grasp of biblical content to challenge those who quote scriptures in support of their own viewpoint. As a result, while some professional theologians have risen to question the movement, most Christians have chosen an uneasy and insecure silence, or have adopted a tolerant live-and-let-live attitude based on traditional American pluralism.

Neither is an adequate response. The Moral Majority and its allies are too intent on capturing the public environment of America to be ignored. It is time for other American Christians to understand what the New Right has in mind for us all, to hold that vision up to the light of our understanding and our faith, and to speak up clearly when we believe they are wrong. That is the purpose and intent of this book.

## The View from the Right

The distinction between viewpoints which seek authority from the past and those which accept change to accommodate the future is as old as biblical religion. In Jesus' time the Jewish people were divided between the Pharisees, whose vision of Judaism had evolved over the years in response to perceived changes in their world, and the Sadducees, who clung tenaciously to the old and unchanging ways of their ancestors. The two groups differed, for example, over the question of resurrection. The Sadducees held the conservative belief that since it was not mentioned in the Law of Moses, it was alien to Judaism. The Pharisees, with whom Jesus sided on this issue, had incorporated belief in resurrection into their religious faith.

Similar distinctions have always divided Christians. In the first century, the conservative Jewish Christians insisted that gentile converts must become Jews and keep the Jewish Law, while Paul and his associates argued that in Christ a new order had begun and that therefore gentiles ought to be accepted freely by the church.

We tend to label those most concerned about maintaining tradition from time past as *conservatives,* while those who choose to accept change are called *liberals* (or *radicals* if they seem to be attacking the foundation on which the tradition is built). But the labels are often misleading, since every tradition begins in change. Most of us are conservative in that we live by preconceptions passed down from those who have gone before. The institutions which shape our civilization came into being long ago—in some cases, such as the family or the church, their origins go back many centuries or even into the dim time of prehistory.

We Americans may find it difficult to recall that our own national identity, colored as it is with the patina of venerability as if it had always been there, had its birth in a violent revolution which shook the whole Western world with its audacity. Those most honored of conservatives, the Founding Fathers, are remembered precisely because they dared to overthrow the existing political institutions and make up new ones out of their creative imaginations. Such awareness ought to make us cautious about the way we use words like *liberal* and *conservative.*

People who describe themselves as *conservatives* sometimes have something slightly different in mind. Often they mean that what matters to them—their most basic beliefs and the values they live by—belong to an order of reality that is *given,* whether by God or historical circumstances. They claim that their principles are guaranteed by an objective validity or truth. Living sucessfully, then, as individuals and in community, consists of recognizing those eternal truths and putting them into practice. But such people are rarely satisfied that their principles are carried out as they ought to be. Generally they look back to some time in the past when their ideals seem to have been more fully realized. The ancient Jews harked back to the time of David, so that when they imagined a future like the "good old days," they always spoke of bringing back those glorious memories. The Book of Acts tells a story of the earliest years of the church when it was energetic, dynamic, and largely undisturbed by the quarrels to which Christians of a later time grew accustomed. No wonder the early church seems like a golden age. Those of us who grew up in the South know that the antebellum world of old Dixie exercised enormous charm for people who knew the harsh aftermath of the Civil War and who overlooked the slavery, poverty, and other aspects of what had gone before. A woman who lived through the blitz in London once told me that they were the best years of her life, because everyone cared about one another and shared in a common purpose. The long nights of terror and the bombs were forgotten; what she recalled was a time in which the anxieties of everyday life faded and a clearly defined reason for living prevailed. Television dramas like "Hogan's Heroes" even find humor and warmth in remembering Nazi prisoner-of-war camps.

I suppose that we all know that the "good old days" were never quite as we imagine them. Paul's letters give a much more human description of the first years of the church than the rosy memories of the Book of Acts; *Gone with the Wind* is fiction after all. Images of the past inevitably tend towards unreality. Yet they are very important for us, because our ancestry (including our spiritual ancestry) does indeed help shape our identity. People without a past are rootless and frightened; lacking a sense of where they came from, they are prisoners of the present moment.

Like every people, Americans have wavered between facing the future as the earth's innovators by experimenting with new ways of being and doing, and clinging to the past because we care so much for what it has given us. Any nation's story could be written in terms of the interplay between liberals and conservatives, and most of us can find traces of both attitudes in ourselves.

The same could be said about any religious tradition, and certainly of American Christianity. Christian faith has not been untouched by its transplantation to American soil, and it has taken on the diversity of the peoples who comprise our population. Yet the dominant, and peculiarly American, strain of Christianity begins with the Puritans of New England and their effort to carve out a new Christian commonwealth in what seemed to them an empty wilderness. On one hand, their impulse was a radical one; they set out to do something no one had ever done before. Yet their guide was their understanding of the teachings of the Bible, and they argued that no source other than the Christian scriptures was of any use in shaping society. Hence their enterprise, unique as it was, sprang from profoundly conservative intentions.

Historians of American society have been aware for a long time of the effects of the interplay between conservative and liberal impulses in our history. The New Right in America must be understood as part of that lengthy tradition. As the next chapter will point out, many of the attitudes of the New Right are as old as this country. Yet if its platform were put into practice, it would profoundly change the institutions and values of American society. For that reason, many claim that the New Right is more radical than conservative. Even its own advocates are sometimes willing to agree: "We are different from previous generations of conservatives. We are no longer working to preserve the status quo. We are radicals, working to overturn the present power structure in this country." [2]

It is nevertheless true that the American New Right describes itself as a conservative movement. Whatever the variations of style and even belief among its advocates, there is also a clear image of what America ought to be. That vision is described by its adherents in terms of principles on which they believe the United States, its institutions and its culture, came into being.

The religious New Right, with which this book is chiefly concerned, is only a part of the flourishing right wing of the

American social and political spectrum. However, it is an important and even crucial part of the movement as a whole, because the principles on which the New Right bases its program are religious principles. Its hopes for America presuppose a religious understanding of the American identity. The United States, in Falwell's view, is "a nation that was founded upon Christian principles, and we have enjoyed a unique relationship with God because of that foundation." [3]

Most of all, the vision of the New Right is a *complete worldview*. It is a coherent whole, providing an all-encompassing set of moral values, a political philosophy, a religious perspective, and a prescribed social structure—a complete culture—which hangs together, and from which nothing can be removed or altered without causing the whole to collapse. Perhaps this is the most significant aspect of the movement. It offers a total way of understanding and living in the world in which there are no loose ends, no uncertainties, no unanswered questions. No doubt this coherence is part of its appeal.

But while the vision of America which the New Right proclaims is a unity, it is nevertheless based on a number of principles which hold the movement together and dictate its program. It is to these that we now turn, in order to complete our picture of this new-old phenomenon of American politics and religion.

### "A Nation under God"

The Puritans' certainty that the settlement of America was undertaken with God's blessing lives on among the advocates of the New Right. Like those hearty settlers, they understand America's identity in terms of its mission as a "light to the nations," demonstrating a commonwealth based on God's law and commending itself to the world by the obvious blessing which would come to such a state. The New Right perceives that divine mission to have come to fruition in American independence and its aftermath, and attributes the rise of the

United States to international preeminence as the direct result of God's blessing. Falwell writes:

> Our Founding Fathers separated church and state in function, but never intended to establish a government void of God. As is evidenced by our Constitution, good people in America must exert an influence and provide a conscience and climate of morality in which it is difficult to go wrong, not difficult for people to go right in America.

> I am positive in my belief regarding the Constitution that God led in the development of that document, and as a result, we here in America have enjoyed 204 years of unparalleled freedom.[4]

> I believe that America has reached the pinnacle of greatness unlike any nation in human history because our Founding Fathers established America's laws and precepts on the principles recorded in the laws of God, including the Ten Commandments.[5]

The religious principles on which the movement is based are not only biblical but clearly Christian. As Falwell comments, "Any diligent student of American history finds that our great nation was founded by godly men upon godly principles to be a Christian nation. Our Founding Fathers were not all Christians, but they were guided by biblical principles."[6]

This religious, and indeed Christian, conception of American identity means that the prosperity and even survival of our nation depends upon the fulfillment of God's intentions for America. Such a view of the national vocation depends upon the clarity of the divine commandments. The Christian Right insists that as the Word of God, the Bible is the only source of information about God's intentions for America and the whole world. It is perceived as an unerring record of the past, "absolutely infallible, without error in all matters pertaining to faith and practice, as well as in areas such as geography, science, history, etc.,"[7]—and also as the medium through which God expresses his intentions for the present and the future. Hence the movement forms part of the *fundamentalist* Christian heritage which has always been part of American Protestantism.

## God's Plans for America

What does American society look like in God's intentions? The New Right has no hesitation in painting a clear picture based on its reading of history as illuminated by the Bible.

The New Right takes freedom with absolute seriousness, but defines it closely. Given the natural human tendency towards sin, there is a need for the rule of law which deters crime by swift and suitable punishment and which should be based on the values confirmed by the Bible. This function of government—"to protect the lives, the liberties, and the property of the citizens"[8]—has its basis in biblical religion. "The role of government is to minister justice and to protect the rights of its citizens by being a terror to evildoers within and without the nation."[9] The state has no other function; within the framework of the law, "individuals should be free to build their own lives without interference from government."[10]

The economic system consistent with such government is unregulated free enterprise. The religious New Right considers America's traditional economic system to follow directly from the biblical imperative that we earn our bread by the sweat of our brow. As Falwell observes, "[God] was giving us the principles of reward for work. The principles established by Almighty God work in every area of our lives."[11] The right to acquire property is a corollary of this principle, and it is government's duty to safeguard that right. Economic policies of the last fifty years, beginning with the New Deal, are therefore judged not only as unwise economically but as morally wrong. Both the growth of the functions of government and its efforts at ameliorating poverty are perceived as immoral since they intrude on individual freedom and attempt to create social change. United States Senator Jesse Helms traces this trend to the decline of faith: "When you have men who no longer believe that

God is in charge of human affairs, you have men attempting to take the place of God by means of the Superstate. The Divine Providence on which our forefathers relied has been supplanted by the Providence of the All-Powerful State."[12] Or as Falwell summarizes recent social discontent: "The pattern is fitting together that when men take their eyes off the principles in the Word of God, there is trouble in every area."[13]

The New Right fears that policies of the recent past have tended to establish the government as the primary institution of society. This they consider counter to God's plan, which bases all human social organization in the *family*.

The model of the family as it is proclaimed by the Moral Majority is worth noting.

> Scripture declares that God has called the father to be the spiritual leader in his family. The husband is not to be the dictator of the family, but the spiritual leader. . . . Good husbands who are godly men are good leaders. Their wives and children want to follow them and be under their protection. The husband is to be the decision-maker and the one who motivates his family with love. The Bible says that husbands are to love their wives even as Christ also loved the Church and gave Himself for it. A man is to be a servant to his family while at the same time being a leader. A husband and father is first of all to be a provider for his family. He is to take care of their physical needs and do this honestly by working and earning an income to meet those needs. Then he is to be a protector. He is to protect them not only from physical harm but from spiritual harm as well.[14]

In sum, it is the task of the father to exercise authority in the communication of what are understood to be proper values, and to do so firmly. "Because we have weak men we have weak homes. . . ."[15]

Nowhere does the New Right perceive a greater threat than to this perception of the "ideal" American family. The enemies are strong and many in number. Government itself bears much of the blame, particularly for fostering an educational system which substitutes "humanist" or "socialist" values for biblical principles. By removing all opportunities for religious practice from the public school system, the State has allied itself with those forces which are fighting against God's intentions for the family.

There are other cultural forces at work to destroy the biblical model of the family. Chief among these is the feminist movement, which avowedly undertakes to promote relations between the sexes based on equality rather than hierarchy. For the New Right, the assertion of women's rights has deformed the God-given social and economic system, leading countless women to abandon their responsibilities as homemakers and mothers in favor of economic success and the desire for material gain. Their absence from the home means that children are left alone at critical formative stages of their growth, and that secular or governmental institutions (schools and day-care centers) are permitted to take over the nurture of America's children.

Another perceived threat to the integrity of the family as the basic social unit is the growing visibility of homosexuals, the emergence of a point of view which describes homosexuality as an alternative life-style, and efforts to guarantee civil rights for homosexuals. The New Right's attitude is based on its conviction that the Bible condemns homosexual behavior, and that so-called gay rights support sexual relationships which are outside, and therefore inimical to, marriage. Furthermore, many of the Right's advocates seem convinced that public acceptance of homosexuality will lead to its increase and that homosexuals in positions of authority pose a threat to children's normal sexual development.

All public display or approval of sexuality outside the confines of marriage is conceived as part of a cultural attack on the family. Such implied approval of sex outside marriage and the relativizing of the institution of marriage are to be found in theater, television, popular music, and the media—most of all in the proliferation of pornography and popular literature which espouses free expression of sexuality, "tells you to do anything you want and then also tells you how to get rid of your guilt when you do it." [16]

Perhaps the issue which arouses most passion and support for the religious New Right is the social and political conflict surrounding the issue of abortion. The New Right defines all abortion as murder, and sees the increasing public acceptance, and even funding, of the termination of pregnancy as a threat to America's future. Says Falwell, "If we expect God to honor and bless our nation, we must take a stand against abortion." [17]

The social and economic perspective espoused by the New Right is a significant part of our cultural heritage, as the next chapter will demonstrate. Its hopes for America are understood to be God-given, unassailable and self-evident. Challenging or questioning them is immoral and risks God's judgment. The New Right's enemies are also enemies of God.

## Knowing the Enemy

For many years the Right has identified Communism as the chief adversary of God's plans for America. The enemy is incarnate in the Soviet Union and other Communist states, and pervades the world of ideas through the subversive philosophy of Marxism-Leninism. As the heirs of McCarthyism, advocates of the New Right tend to interpret many or all attacks on their image of America as evidence of hidden Communism. Marxism is conceived not so much as an alternative economic or political theory as an alien theology (or atheology, since its world view is materialist and atheist by definition). To the Moral Majority, the real threat of Communism lies in its anti-God stance. As Falwell states, "When communism takes over a nation, the first thing that happens is that the churches are shut down, preachers are killed or imprisoned, and Bibles are taken away from the people." [18] The Communist hostility to America stems, in Falwell's view, from our *religious* mission: "Evil forces," he writes, "would seek to destroy America because she is a bastion for Christian missions and a base for world evangelization."[19]

This attack is furthered by the undermining of traditional American values, since "Communists know that in order to take over a country they must first see to it that a nation's military strength is weakened and that its morals are corrupted so that its people will have no will to resist wrong."[20]

No duty lies more heavily upon our government than strong resistance to the Communist threat; hence "the bearing of the sword by the government is correct and proper. Nowhere in the Bible is there a rebuke for the bearing of armaments. A political leader, as a minister of God, is a revenger to execute wrath upon those who do evil."[21]

In fact, the New Right perceives a decline in American willingness to fight for its principles as a significant sign of the immorality of recent governmental posture. Efforts to reduce arms and achieve cutbacks in military spending are described as foolish and wrong, an abdication of the state's God-given obligation to provide security for its people against an enemy perceived in demonic terms.

In the struggle between the forces of God and the legions of evil, others intentionally or unwittingly help erode American strength and will, chief among them the *secular humanists*. The New Right understands humanism as a coherent and hostile world view which threatens the Right's image of America by pursuing alternative values and interpretations of the nature and function of our institutions. Humanism is described as a godless perspective which substitutes tolerance for Christian absolutes. Humanists see America as a mosaic of many religions and value systems and seek to find means by which all can coexist and cooperate in creating a national identity. To the Moral Majority, the secular humanist's tolerance is the logical outcome of American liberalism, and cannot but destroy the principles on which their image of America rests. The New Right believes that the American educational system, bureaucracy and government, its intellectuals and its advocates are united in a point of view which will undermine the very basis of American society if it is permitted to prevail. Falwell warns: "As the Bible and prayer were removed [from the schools] they were replaced with courses reflecting the philosophy of humanism. . . . Humanists believe that man is his own god and that moral values are relative, that ethics are situational. Humanists say that the Ten Commandments and other moral and ethical laws are 'outmoded' and hindrances to human progress. . . . The attitude America's people take toward the Bible is in direct proportion to the stability of America as a nation." [22]

The Christian Right has come to understand the traditional doctrine of separation of church and state as a means by which opponents of their view have pressed their attack. One Baptist pastor writes:

> We have been so intimidated that under the guise of separation of Church and State we silently watch our nation's Judeo-Christian roots being torn out. Our legal system, historically and constitutionally moored to the biblical standards of morality highlighted in the Ten Commandments, has been assaulted by the amoral, situational morality of humanists while we sat back making sure we did not infringe on the separation of Church and State as taught to us by the secularists. While we faithfully marched to the secularist's drumbeat of separation of Church and State, our public schools were flushed of anything God-Fearing, pro-moral or pro-American. Pumped in was a host of camouflages for the humanist's atheistic assaults on captive and impressionable minds of the young. Thus we live in the midst of moral decadence, economic chaos and military demise. [23]

Believing that it had been misled into silence, the Christian New Right has entered the political arena to do battle on behalf of its vision of a godly America. Falwell's organization, Moral Majority, Inc., is only the best known of many groups which have opted for the political fray. Many of the most visible are formed around a single issue, such as opposition to abortion or gun control. They have sought to exert their influence in several ways, including endorsement and financial backing for political candidates who support their point of view, and designating hostile incumbents for defeat. The National Pro-Life Political Action Committee announced as early as June of 1981 its plan to commit $650,000 to defeat a "target list" of four senators and five representatives in the 1982 elections because they do not support antiabortion legislation. The committee indicated its intention "to influence those congressmen, senators and candidates from both parties who are ambivalent or undecided on this matter of life versus death."[24] Moral Majority, Inc., began well more than a year in advance of those elections to conduct political leadership training sessions for grass-roots organizing.[25] As Falwell observes:

> Christians must keep America great by being willing to go into the halls of Congress, by getting laws passed that will protect the freedom and liberty of her citizens. The Moral Majority, Inc. was formed to acquaint Americans everywhere with the tragic decline in our nation's morals and to provide leadership in establishing an effective coalition of morally active citizens who are (a) prolife, (b) profamily, (c) promoral, and (d) pro-American. If the vast majority of Americans . . . still believe the Ten Commandments are valid today, why are we permitting a few leading amoral humanists and naturalists to take over the most influential positions in this nation?[26]

What is called for is nothing less than a crusade—a crusade to save America.

> [I]t will not be long before we are in a hell very much of our own making. But whether the end comes with a bang or a whimper, we are nearly at our corporate Point of No Return, beyond which it will be too late for America, as a nation, to turn back.

> Yet such is God's mercy, that He does not even require the whole nation to repent. It is enough if only the Christians, those

who truly know Him, will do this. . . . America would yet become the citadel of light which God intended her to be from the beginning![27]

## God's Warriors

The New Right has no hesitation about its use of the word *Christian* to describe not only individuals but points of view, policy decisions, and courses of action. Its meaning, however, may be considerably more restrictive than might be obvious. Challenged by a Jewish inquirer about Christian anti-Semitism as exhibited in the Spanish Inquisition, the Reverend Dan Fore, head of the New York branch of Moral Majority, replied, "Those weren't Christians, they were Roman Catholics."[28]

The Christians of the New Right are in fact drawn primarily from the ranks of American Protestantism, especially from the independent congregations and fundamentalist denominations which rely almost entirely on a narrowly conservative reading of the Bible for their theology. Their attitude towards the mainline Protestant denominations tends towards scorn and disdain, since they see the churches' leadership in bondage to the liberal and humanist forces who have done so much to undermine their image of America. A strong antielitist sentiment toward those perceived to form the "liberal establishment" leads the New Right to view the clergy and theologians identified with that establishment not as potential allies but as the enemy.

Leadership of the Christian New Right rests in the hands of men and a very few women who are reminiscent of the fundamentalist evangelists who have always been part of the American religious community. However, they have achieved a notoriety, and perhaps a measure of influence, undreamed of by earlier generations of popular preachers. This success is directly related to their discovery of the power of the media, especially television, and skilled use of computerized mass mailing for mobilizing public opinion and fund raising.

Early estimates, particularly those suggested by the television preachers themselves, portrayed many millions of Americans as regular or occasional viewers of New Right broadcasting. Ben Armstrong's 1979 book *The Electronic Church* asserted that nearly 130 million Americans view the programming. Estimates in the news media credited the preachers with audiences of 40 to 50 million. Falwell claims a weekly audience of between 17 and 25 million. Several recent studies indicate that the numbers are much lower. Arbitron, a television research organization cited in a 1981 study entitled *Prime Time Preachers,* indicates that between 1977 and 1980 the weekly audience declined from 21 to 20 million viewers. The A. C. Nielson Company's *Report on Syndicated Programs* for February and November, 1980, indicates that only two of the top ten independent television preachers reached as many as 2 percent of the households in areas to which their programs are broadcast. During a typical month fewer than 10 million households watched even one of the ten preachers. Falwell draws a weekly audience of nearly 1.5 million. (Arbitron's study shows Falwell's audience growing by 13 percent between 1979 and 1980, while Nielson reports a slight decline during a similar period.)[29]

Whatever the numbers of their supporters, it is clear that the preachers of the Christian Right occupy a position from which they can shape public opinion and also have access to significant financial backing.

Richard Viguerie, head of his own fund-raising firm, RAVCO of Falls Church, Virginia, has emerged as the chief technician of mass advertising as a political and religious tool of the New Right. Author of a book entitled *The New Right: We're Ready to Lead,* Viguerie has compiled a series of interlocking mailing lists from which he solicits funding for the candidates and groups who are his clients. His firm now possesses "3000 reels of magnetic computer tape containing the names and addresses of more than 10 percent of the population of the United States," and mails "100 million pieces of mail a year from some 300 mailing lists that contain the names of 25 million Americans."[30]

Using a combination of mass mailing and television soliciting, Falwell's organization, "The Old-Time Gospel Hour," raised
$115 million between 1977 and 1980. Some $16 million of this
sum went into construction of Liberty Baptist College, with an
additional $2 million yearly for the college's operating expenses;
most of the money, however, was spent for the television broadcasting.[31]

Many of the television appeals for funds imply that viewers'
contributions will be used for specific projects: a clinic in Mex-
ico built by Robert Schuller's "Hour of Power," missionary activity in Central America among refugees (Jimmy Swaggert
Ministries), and in Honduras to "fight Communism" (Pat Robertson's "700 Club").[32] At the same time, many imply that the
survival of their programming depends upon generous contributions. Jim Bakker, host of the "PTL Club," a Christian variety show, requests monthly pledges from his viewers and also
appeals for special fifty-dollar gifts.[33]

Broad support from many viewers accounts for the huge sums
of money available to the New Right. Viguerie and others have
access to some foundations and individuals like the Sarah Scaife
Family Charitable Trust and Colorado brewer Joseph Coors.[34]
The director of financial development for Moral Majority reminds fund raisers that "there are people who have the ability to
give more than you've ever dreamed of in your life."[35] But most
of the funding for the religious New Right is derived from the
effective soliciting of contributions in small amounts from large
numbers of supporters. Contributors are drawn largely from the
ranks of white, working- and lower-middle-class Americans,
most of whom live in the South and West. The New Right
aims its appeals at those who feel themselves alienated from
those perceived to hold political, economic, or cultural power
(the "elite" or "establishment") and also differentiate themselves
sharply from those whom they regard as beneficiaries of the
"welfare state." Kevin Phillips, himself one of its chief political
strategists, notes that the emergence of the New Right is "a

populist revolt of the American masses who have been elevated by prosperity to middle-class status and conservatism. *Their* revolt is against the caste, policies and taxation of the mandarins of Establishment liberalism." [36] The religious New Right represented by the Moral Majority and similar organizations is the Protestant wing of a coalition of the like-minded. One of the significant factors in the contemporary aspect of the Right is a new willingness on the part of conservative Protestants to forge tactical, single-issue-oriented alliances with other religious groups for reasons of political strategy. The Protestant Right has historically been wary of all religious traditions different from its own. The proximity of American Judaism and Roman Catholicism has done little to temper that prejudice. Asked by a Jewish interviewer, "As a Jew, if I don't accept Christ, I'll go to hell?" the Moral Majority's Dan Fore replied, "Yes, but it's nothing personal or unique to Jews. The same goes for the Chinese, the Moslems, everyone. . . ." [37]

Nevertheless, in the changed political climate of the 1980s, the religious New Right has come to realize the potential strength of alliances with conservatives of other religious allegiances. Falwell goes so far as to observe, "I admire the courage the Catholics have shown down through the centuries in standing against abortion. There have been times when they have had to stand alone." [38] But there are limits to such alliances, and the New Right seeks no allies who do not share its preconceptions. In Falwell's words: "As a fundamental, independent, separatist Baptist, I am well aware of the crucial issues of personal and ecclesiastical separation that divide fundamentalists philosophically from evangelicals and liberals. I do not believe that it is ever right to compromise the truth in order to gain an opportunity to do right. In doctrinal and spiritual matters, there is no real harmony between light and darkness." [39]

Perhaps that comment can serve as the summary to this description of the Christian Right. It sees the world as a battleground between two absolutes, God and evil, and Christians know which side they are on. No skirmish holds any ambiguity or room for doubt; all is light and darkness, and the only choice that matters is which side we are on. It is a vision of the world, and of Americans and American Christians in the world, as warriors for the right—and for the Right. It is an image of reality painted with broad strokes and clear alternatives. To those who have been captivated by its charms and promises, it is a way of life which holds out certainty in exchange for faithfulness.

But there are questions to be asked. Does the Christian Right really preach the faith passed down to us from the time of Christ? Are its priorities in fact those of the Bible and of the Christian Church? Is its ethical stance that of the apostles and prophets? Is the church as the Moral Majority describes it? Is the truth so simple and so overwhelming? Certainly Christians on the Right have no doubts about these matters. I for one am not so sure.

# Looking Backward

## The New Israel

No doubt the Puritan colonists who first established settlements in New England looked on the American wilderness as a providential sanctuary after years of hostility and persecution in their native England. As they reflected upon their vain hope to create in England a commonwealth in accordance with their reading of the scriptures and Geneva's John Calvin, they must have been grateful for a refuge thousands of miles from their failure. But if we may trust their own writings, such emotions pale beside the more optimistic attitude they brought with them to these shores. Untouched by the institutions of European society and sparsely populated by a people they intended to convert or ignore, America was more than a refuge. It was a God-given opportunity to do what they had never been able to accomplish in the Old World: to establish a society which would be built entirely on their understanding of God's Law as revealed in the Bible. They set out to "make over a portion of the earth in the spirit of Christian philosophy: a new church and state, family and school, ethic and conduct. They might and did differ among themselves as to the realization of those high and holy aims; but a new City of God was their aim."[1]

The Puritans undertook their venture with the certainty that it was God's will for them, and therefore confidently expecting God's blessing in return for their obedience. Nor did they conceive their undertaking simply for their own benefit. Rather, it was God's opportunity, and theirs, to demonstrate to the whole world how a truly Christian society would look; and like all missionaries, they trusted that because their enterprise would enjoy God's unprecedented blessing, it would attract converts by its own merits. How, they asked themselves, could anyone fail to prefer such a state as they would build? They were certain too that not only human eyes were watching; God would also have an eye on them, and they assumed that if they abandoned the principles on which they were building, God's blessing would be lifted and their venture would fail—insuring their own destruction and also hindering God's efforts to use them as an example. These thoughts form the burden of a well-known sermon preached by John Winthrop to a shipful of colonists on board the *Arrabella* as they prepared to land in Massachusetts in 1630:

> Thus stands the cause between God and us: we are entered into covenant with Him for this work. . . . We shall find that the God of Israel is among us, when ten of us shall be able to resist a thousand of our enemies, when He shall make us a praise and glory, that men of succeeding plantations shall say, 'The Lord make it like that of New England'. For we must consider that we shall be as a City upon a Hill, the eyes of all people are upon us. . . .[2]

Steeped as they were in the language and imagery of the Bible, it is not surprising that those Puritan settlers interpreted their own story in terms of the history of Israel. Like the Israelites, they had endured persecution and exile; they had passed across the sea to a new land of promise; they conceived of their relationship with God as a covenant which would bring blessing and favor in return for faithfulness. Like Israel, the Puritans interpreted the events of their life as signs of the constant presence and attention of a God favorably disposed towards them and intervening on their behalf in mercy and judgment. The slightest evidence of good fortune seemed to carry with it a hint of God's special favor. Cotton Mather, well-known Puritan cleric, compiled and published hundreds of pages of evidence of God's special providence as shown towards the New Englanders.

> For instance, an honest carpenter being at a work upon a house where eight children were sitting in a ring at some childish play on the floor below; he let fall accidentally from an upper floor a bulky piece of timber just over these little children. The good man, with inexpressible agony, cried out, 'O Lord, direct it'! and the Lord did so direct it that it fell on end of the midst of the little children and then canted along the floor between two of the children, without touching one of them all. But the instances of such things would be numberless.[3]

On the other hand, the Puritans were equally certain that sin would be swiftly punished by a just God; John Winthrop observed that the accidental drowning of two servants of a Mr. Moody of Roxbury was in fact God's judgment, for "they were wicked persons."[4]

It follows, then, that the remedy for disaster when sin has come to pass is repentance. As Marshall and Manuel comment: "That a drought could be broken, or an Indian attack averted, by corporate repentance is an idea which sounds alien to many Christians today. Yet it was central to the faith which built this country. . . ."[5]

The stern faithfulness of the Puritan settlers mellowed or declined over the years into a less rigorous, more formalized style of Christianity. It has left its mark on our language with the adjective *puritanical,* which has come to denote a smug, pleasure-denying, austere, and often self-righteous style of living and believing, perhaps best described in Nathaniel Hawthorne's novel *The Scarlet Letter* or Arthur Miller's drama *The Crucible.* But there is more to their legacy than that stereotype. Although few Americans would find themselves attracted to the Puritans' brand of Christianity, most have probably lived all their lives with assumptions inherited from them. In particular, the notion of America as the Promised Land and of Americans as God's Chosen People has come to permeate our national consciousness. Robert Bellah describes these beliefs as central to what he calls our "civil religion," a way of understanding our national identity as sacred and purposeful.[6]

Americans have commonly understood their national purpose in terms of a mission to the rest of the world. Our War of Independence was an example to other oppressed peoples; we entered the First World War to "make the world safe for democracy"; we have fought the Nazis and the Communists not only for our own survival but on behalf of the free world as part of our God-given mission. It is doubtful if America has ever given up its sense of calling as a "light to the nations." For better or worse, it has passed into the hearts and minds of most Americans, and it illuminates the thoughts, words, and deeds of people who would be amazed to learn that it all began with the Puritans. Bellah writes, "The obligation, both collective and individual, to carry out God's will on earth . . . was the motivating spirit of those who founded America, and it has been present in every generation since."[7]

Even the cultured and sophisticated thinkers whose work lies behind the documents of American independence, and who would, for the most part, have disdained the Puritans as dour and superstitious, took for granted that God has a special interest in America; they too understood their work to be a God-given commission. Not since Joshua, proclaimed Congregationalist preacher Ezra Stiles in 1789, had such a divinely-appointed warrior as Washington appeared to lead God's people.[8]

It seems clear that America has never abandoned that sense of national purpose and destiny which it interprets in sacred terms. The experiment in freedom and the principles of democracy tentatively explored in the Declaration of Independence and the Constitution stand not on their own terms or merits but as signs of God's will. Thomas Jefferson and other authors of those documents would never have dared to set down such thoughts if they had not been convinced that they were doing so with God's blessing.

## Revival

It is probably true that no people have ever had a stronger sense of their own individual duty and call than the Puritans of New England. The inner certainty of God's election gave them at once enormous confidence and deep commitment. The longing for certainty and listening for the voice of God within them survived even the decline of Puritanism and its dilution by other, less rigorous, styles of faith which were brought to America.

During the 1730s and continuing for many years, a movement known as the "Great Awakening" spread rapidly along the eastern seaboard bringing revival and a new American style to Christian faith. Distressed by the cold rigidity to which Puritanism had declined, clergy and lay people proclaimed that if only believers would open themselves fully to God's call, the Spirit would convey a powerful, often dramatic, testimony to God's entrance into the life and awareness of the individual Christian. As people began to exhibit these potent "conversions," they interpreted them as being "born again" as Jesus had commanded Nicodemus;[9] many considered the Awakening as a portent of the "last days" prophesied in the Book of Revelation. As the movement overflowed the settled areas of the East Coast, it was transformed into a highly emotional style of Christianity which sought above all else the affirmation of God's call and the individual believer's faithful response. The ability to preach in such a way as to induce the experience of conversion and repentance overshadowed other pastoral gifts, and people took to the pulpit out of inner compulsion, regardless of training or ecclesiastical approval. The academic pursuit of theology seemed dry and moribund in comparison with the lively and energetic practice of a Christianity which could produce outbursts of "spirit" and zeal. What more could anyone need than a simple trust in the Bible as the Word of God and in Christ as the sacrifice for sin? The disputes of centuries seemed trivial and beyond the understanding of Christians on the frontier, who had no time or opportunity for schooling of any kind. The Great Awakening brought to American Christianity simplicity, fundamentalism, a democratic style which minimized distinctions between clergy and laity, sporadic interest in the imminent Second Coming of Christ, and passionate preaching to induce ecstasy, repentance, and changed lives. Not surprisingly, the evidence of the reality of conversion could be expected to manifest itself in obedience to God's laws; but the frontier had no interest in the niceties of civil government as Massachusetts had developed it. What mattered where people were scattered widely in rugged and hostile territory were the virtues of survival: faithfulness, trustworthiness, self-reliance, sobriety. By the time the Great Awakening had run its course, American religion was permanently divided between the more structured churches in eastern urban areas and on southern plantations, and a new-style, freewheeling, simplified, and highly emotional brand of Christianity adapted for the frontier.

The Great Awakening was followed some years later by another similar movement, known as the Second Awakening, which began at the turn of the nineteenth century. Most denominations felt something of its influence, and "revivalism in its many forms was the most powerful force in nineteenth century Protestant life."[10] On the frontier, it gave birth to an indigenous form of American religious institution, the camp meeting. Families who lived many miles from each other gathered at a central place to camp for many days at a time, in order to listen to an especially skilled preacher who would revive their flagging zeal, induce conversion and repentance as dramatically as possible, and otherwise strengthen the life of faith. Camp meetings were one of the most important forms of institutionalized religion on the American frontier in the nineteenth century. In addition to their obvious religious function, they were also the primary social gathering and provided opportunities for families to be with neighbors, exchange news, and otherwise cement social bonds. As the frontier moved west, the camp meeting went with it and remained throughout the century a potent form of religious revival among people largely alienated from the more formalized religion of the towns and cities.

Frontier preachers, the historian Richard Hofstadter observes, "would have been ineffective had they been the sort of pastors who were appropriate to the settled churches of the East. They would have been ineffective in converting their moving flocks if they had not been able to develop a vernacular style in preaching, and if they had failed to share or to simulate in some degree the sensibilities and prejudices of their audiences—antiauthority, anti-aristocracy, anti-Eastern, anti-learning." [11]

Those attitudes were *cultural* in that they spell out the popular values of the "plain people" of America who looked with hostility upon the educated, urban, largely eastern purveyors of political and economic power in the nineteenth century. As early as 1830, the famous French traveler and observer of America Alexis de Tocqueville noted with concern the cultural divisions among the different regions of the United States. The northern states, early centers of manufacturing, prospered more rapidly than other areas. This fact, coupled with historic differences in values, political and social life, made de Tocqueville worry that the union on which the country was built might be strained to the breaking point. "Thus the prosperity of the United States is the source of their most serious danger, since it tends to create in some of the . . . States that intoxication which accompanies a rapid increase of fortune; and to awaken in others those feelings of envy, mistrust, and regret which usually attend the loss of it." [12]

De Tocqueville also prophesied that eventually the West would rise in power and influence, eclipsing even the Northeast. De Tocqueville wondered if the central government necessary to American survival would survive such factionalism. He was troubled by the election of Andrew Jackson to the presidency in

1829 because Jackson was "placed in this lofty station by the passions which are most opposed to the central government. . . . General Jackson is the slave of the majority. . . ."[13]

No doubt de Tocqueville was troubled by what one historian called Jackson's willingness to provide for many Americans "a moral definition of their situation, construing out of immediate events the great struggle between people and aristocracy for mastery of the republic."[14] Jackson chose to identify "the class enemy as the money power, the moneyed aristocracy, and so forth. . . . Beneath the gross polemical image of people versus aristocracy one finds the steady note of praise for simplicity and stability, self-reliance and independence, economy and useful toil, honesty and plain dealing."[15]

Such divisions and the anxieties which accompany them lie behind what Richard Hofstadter calls a "paranoid style in American politics," based less on actual distinctions in material wealth and power than perceived differences in *status*. As he observed, the United States is "a country in which so many people do not know who they are or what they are or what they belong to or what belongs to them. It is a country of people whose status expectations are random and uncertain, and yet whose status aspirations have been whipped up to a high pitch by our democratic ethos and our rags-to-riches mythology."[16]

### Peoples' Politics, Peoples' Religion

Historians describe the cultural stance which lay behind the election of Andrew Jackson as *populism*. It is "the perennial American 'ism',"[17] and belonged originally to rural or small-town Protestants, passionate in patriotism (and mistrust of people or ideas which seem to be "foreign"), dedicated to the self-reliance essential for survival in most American settings, and determined to make their own way in small business or farming if only the elite whom they understood to control government and commerce would give them a chance.

This populist style has colored American politics and religion for at least a century and a half. It blossomed in fundamentalist preaching (the popular evangelist Dwight L. Moody once remarked, "An educated rascal is the meanest kind of rascal");[18] in violence and hate directed towards the immigrants who flocked to the United States during the nineteenth century and who appeared to threaten both jobs and values hallowed in American tradition; in attacks on Roman Catholicism as an alien and dangerous force through which the pope might well take over America; in fears of complex conspiracies, and in organized racism such as the Ku Klux Klan, which fed on poor whites' fears that blacks, Jews, and Roman Catholics were in an unholy alliance to destroy their way of life.

Probably populism's chief hero is William Jennings Bryan. Bryan rose to national preeminence in the mid-1890s, when a severe depression coupled with a collapse of farm prices drove the unemployment rate up to 20 percent. Bryan supported the populist demand for the free coinage of silver currency as a remedy for the depression, in opposition to the gold standard favored by the banking community, eastern Republicans, and major business interests. One populist tract of the period proclaimed, "The business men of New York City passed strong resolutions against the Declaration of Independence in 1776, and they are passing strong resolutions against an American policy now."[19] Against this background of passion and conflict, Bryan emerged from the United States Senate to run as the Democratic party's presidential candidate in 1896. Although he lost the election, he became the first presidential candidate since Jackson to draw together a coalition of independent farmers and owners of small businesses, "plain people," and fight a presidential campaign on the basis of populist issues.

Bryan was an excellent example of the populist style: born in "an ambiance of rural Protestant evangelism," schooled in the rhetoric of "inspired oratory, laced with biblical allusions, aimed at 'elevating' the audience and transmuting mundane questions of politics and economics into grand moral issues."[20] By the time he appeared on the scene, American populist religion had grasped something of the new threat which the contemporary learning of the day was posing to its most fundamental conceptions of God, the world, and humankind. Hofstadter describes the changed intellectual climate in this way:

> The coming of Darwinism, with its widespread and pervasive influence upon every area of thinking, put orthodox Christianity on the defensive; and the impact of Darwinism was heightened by modern scholarly Biblical criticism among the learned ministry and among educated laymen. Finally, toward the end of the century, the problems of industrialism and the urban churches gave rise to a widespread movement for a social gospel, another modernist tendency. Ministers and laymen alike now had to choose between fundamentalism and modernism; between conservative Christianity and the social gospel.[21]

Among the mainstream denominations, many of the clergy and laity, as well as professional theologians, worked very hard at finding ways of accommodating Christian belief to the new discoveries of science and the theories of social scientists alike. The fundamentalist churches, wedded to their faith in the inerrancy of the Bible, had no such option, and became increasingly shrill as "modern" ideas became more pervasive. By Bryan's time, populists had committed themselves to an antimodernist stance.

Bryan fought for the cause in the 1920s with the same energy he had brought to the political arena: as Hofstadter observed, he "combined in his person the two basic ancestral pieties of the people—evangelical faith and populist democracy."[22] Bryan once proclaimed: "All the ills from which America suffers can be traced back to the teaching of evolution. It would be better to destroy every other book ever written, and save just the first three verses of Genesis."[23]

In 1925, the Tennessee legislature passed a bill outlawing the teaching of evolution in the public schools, on grounds that it would undermine the family. Indeed, its author introduced the bill "because he had heard of a young woman in his own community who had gone to a university and returned an evolutionist. . . . 'Save our children for God'! cried a member of the Tennessee Senate. . . ." Shortly before his death, Bryan assisted the Tennessee attorney general in prosecuting John T. Scopes, a high school biology teacher and the new law's first victim. Bryan declared, "Our purpose and our only purpose is to vindicate the right of parents to guard the religion of their children. . . ."[24]

Bryan's role in the Scopes trial was simply the painful end of a career dedicated to the premise that "social problems are essentially moral—that is to say, religious." In Hofstadter's words, Bryan found it "inconceivable that the hardworking, Bible-reading citizenry should be inferior in moral insight to the cynical financiers of the Eastern cities. Because they were, as Bryan saw it, better people, they were better moralists, and hence better economists. In after years when he bustled the support of the anti-evolution laws with the argument that he was defending the democracy of Tennessee, he was simply carrying this variety of political primitivism to its logical end."[25]

Hofstadter observes that status politics is often more concerned to support values and emotions than actions; it is more likely to *oppose* than to *devise* programs.[26] One exception was the movement supporting the prohibition of alcoholic beverages. No issue except evolution so clearly united the religious and political impulses of populist America. Although early accounts of American life leave no doubt that our ancestors consumed alcohol in prodigious amounts, its use was condemned by many progressives in the nineteenth century because of its effect on social and family well-being. Frontier preachers often identified "demon rum" as one of the chief means by which the devil works his will on unsuspecting sinners; and it is understandable that in the rugged and hardworking environment of the American West, alcohol could be seen as the companion of violence, lethargy, and sloth. In the popular mind, alcohol was associated with those elements from which they were most alienated: the urban and cosmopolitan, the rich—and the immigrant. The passage of the Volstead Act in 1919, following a constitutional amendment approved earlier that year, prohibited the sale of all beverages containing more than half of one percent alcohol. It represents one of the very few political victories in which a specifically populist program (not, by the way, based on the Bible) was established as national policy. Its repeal only fourteen years later indicates that the cultural values on which it was based did not, and could not, command broad allegiance from an American society already permanently pluralistic.

Twentieth-century populism has been fed by a volatile blend of powerlessness and militance. The perspective and identity it creates can be seen clearly in a 1926 statement by the Imperial Wizard of the Ku Klux Klan.

> We are a movement of the plain people, very weak in the matter of culture, intellectual support, and trained leadership. We are demanding, and we expect to win, a return of power into the hands of the everyday, not highly cultured, not overly intellectualized, but entirely unspoiled and not de-Americanized, average citizen of the old stock. . . .
>
> This is undoubtedly a weakness. It lays us open to the charge of being 'hicks' and 'rubes' and 'drivers of secondhand Fords.' We admit it. Far worse, it makes it hard for us to state our case and advocate our crusade in the most effective way, for most of us lack skill in language. . . .
>
> The Klan does not believe that the fact that it is emotional and instinctive, rather than coldly intellectual, is a weakness. . . .[27]

Certainly not all those who identified with populist concerns succumbed to the Klan, but this statement indicates clearly some of the tendencies of the populists' vision of America: patriotism which can spill over into prejudice, indifference towards reason, hints of racism which can be ignited easily into hatred.

Ironically, in the 1930s and again in the 1950s, it was Roman Catholics who spoke for the populists' discontent and served as its focus. In the 1930s, the Reverend Charles Coughlin became one of the first preachers to utilize radio, mobilizing wide support by attacking big business, eastern intellectuals, and policies he suspected of aiding countries other than the United States (he also ventured into electoral politics). Father Coughlin's appeal was somewhat limited by his religion—which made him suspect to many fundamentalist Protestants—and by indigenous southern political figures like Huey Long with whom he had to compete.

In the early 1950s, Senator Joseph R. McCarthy of Wisconsin became the spearhead of a broad attack on what he claimed was a monumental infiltration of Communists into every corner of American life: government, the universities, the entertainment industry, the media. It is interesting from the perspective of the history of populism that McCarthy considered the affluent elite as the chief dwelling place of Marxism. As one historian observed, McCarthy "associated Communism with fancy manners, Anglophilism, Harvard, pretensions to high culture, all the qualities that vintage populism had associated with the Eastern Establishment."[28]

Although a Roman Catholic, McCarthy was fluent in the language and themes which fundamentalist preachers had always used in contrasting themselves with their enemies—and God's:

> The great difference between our western Christian world and the atheistic Communist world is not political, ladies and gentlemen, it is moral. . . . The real, basic difference lies in the religion of immoralism—invented by Marx, preached feverishly by Lenin, and carried to unimaginable extremes by Stalin. This religion of immoralism, if the Red half of the world wins— and well it may—this religion of immoralism will more deeply wound and damage mankind than any conceivable economic or political system. . . . Today we are engaged in final, all-out battle between communistic atheism and Christianity.[29]

The John Birch Society and other right-wing groups continued McCarthy's attack on Communism into the 1960s, going even further than he in identifying liberalism with the Communists. (The right-wing radio and television commentator Dan Smoot once remarked, "I equate the growth of the welfare state with Socialism and Socialism with Communism.")[30] In spite of its roots in the black churches, the civil rights movement was perceived by many whites as a radical attack on the structural basis of American society. Their response brought into the open the racist implications of the extreme Right's point of view. Martin Luther King and other leaders of the movement were repeatedly accused of Communist affiliation and backing, and the content of King's "dream" was described as a blueprint for the destruction of God's plans for America.

No one better summed up these attitudes than George Wallace, an Alabama governor with a background in the populist tradition of the South who emerged as the symbol of resistance to racial integration and then went on as a national advocate of many perennial populist concerns. As Wallace proclaimed in his 1972 campaign for the Democratic party's presidential nomination: "Too long this party has been controlled by the so-called intellectual snobs who feel that big government should control the lives of American citizens from the cradle to the grave. . . ."[31] Months later, he wrote: "I want to help the Democratic Party. I want it again to become the party of the average citizen in this country as it used to be, and not the party of the intellectual pseudo-snobbery that has controlled it for so many years."[32]

The phrase "law and order" which became the catchword of Wallace's campaign was itself indicative of his desire to restore America to an image which he saw as under attack—by the affluent young who had benefited from it and yet scorned its traditional values; by those who criticized its behavior in foreign affairs; by those who disdained its traditional social and family patterns; by the federal government; and by those who, ignoring both law and custom, engaged in domestic violence. The rioting which exploded in metropolitan ghettos and the massive antiwar demonstrations of the late 1960s seemed to Wallace and many others a threat to the only America they knew.

Wallace's presidential aspirations were interrupted by an assassination attempt which left him partially disabled. His demise from the political scene left a vacuum which has been filled by a cast of new characters, including tacticians like Howard Phillips, Richard Viguerie, Kevin Phillips, and a number of newly elected political leaders who came to power with the support of the New Right. Their intentions are summed up in the title of Viguerie's 1981 celebration of "conservatism," *The New Right: We're Ready to Lead.* Kevin Phillips, however, admits that much of their perspective "is not conservative so much as populist."[33]

Viguerie is convinced that the New Right is "the most important force to appear in decades."[34] In his introduction to Viguerie's book, Falwell affirms the lineage of their position: The New Right is not really new but comprises "the backbone of our country—those citizens who . . . have integrity and believe in hard work, those who pledge allegiance to the flag, and proudly sing our national anthem . . . who love their country and are willing to sacrifice for her."[35]

In Viguerie's view, the "ready-made network" provided by the numerous conservative radio and television preachers enables the New Right to bypass the "liberal" media. Indeed he is prepared to say that "numerically and perhaps historically, our most important asset is Dr. Jerry Falwell's Moral Majority. The Moral Majority showed the enormous power religious people can have in America. . . . In 1980 alone, the Moral Majority helped 2.5 million voters register for the first time."[36] Viguerie also applauds the work of the Religious Round Table, which, in four months of 1980, sponsored "public affairs briefings" for "approximately 40,000 conservative religious leaders including over 20,000 preachers," who could then return to their congregations and "explain to them the danger America faced from liberals and humanists."[37]

The New Right sees itself at the threshold of power, because it is "in harmony with the deepest sentiments of the American people." [38] And, says Viguerie, "that's why we're a 'menace'. Not a menace to the country. A menace to the status quo." [39] "We in the New Right are young and vigorous . . . The liberals had a lot of victories over the last 50 years. But they've grown soft and sluggish. They have lost confidence in themselves. We're lean, determined and hungry—to gain victories for conservatism and to renew our great country. Yes the tide is turning. It is turning our way—freedom's way." [40]

At their side is a group of preachers ready to stoke the spiritual fires to light their way. In Falwell's words: "The movement made up of conservative Americans can no longer be silenced or ignored. America's destiny awaits its action." [41]

# God and Power

"God said it. I believe it.
And that settles it."
—Bumper Sticker

"Jesus was not a pacifist.
He was not a sissy."
—The Reverend Jerry Falwell[1]

During the early centuries of the church, Christians began to speculate about what Jesus' childhood must have been like. Several anonymous authors set out to remedy the lack of information by creating narratives which they tried to pass off as gospels like those in the New Testament. In their stories, Jesus amuses other children in the neighborhood by molding birds out of clay and setting them loose to fly away; but on another occasion, when he is taunted by his friends, in a fit of pique he strikes them dead.

Needless to say, those "gospels" never found their way into the Bible. The Church always knew the stories were false, because they portray the child Jesus in terms of sheer, naked power untempered by either justice or mercy. The child of those tales is interested only in silencing the scorn of his neighbors, and in demonstrating command over nature merely to impress his audience. The first Christians knew that Jesus would never have done such things. Their experience and memories portrayed a very different Christ, who stood mute before Pilate and did not come down from the cross, and for whom no legions of angels came to the rescue. Rather, the use of power to further his own ends appears in the Gospels as one of the temptations against which Jesus fought throughout his ministry. At the same time, one of the reasons for his popularity was that, unlike the typically cautious, timid religious leader, Jesus spoke and acted *with authority*—so much so that his contemporaries were amazed. Adversaries were silenced, while twisted bodies and minds responded to his word of healing and forgiveness, because it carried with it the sure ring of authority.

## Power and the Right

The Christian Right is very much concerned about authority and its prerogatives. It tends, however, to conceive of authority not in terms of *right* but of *power*. All of life is defined in terms of the tension between power and powerlessness. For the Christian Right, God's primary attribute is, in fact, power; the human response to God is spelled out in terms of obedience. In their writing and sermons, God is described almost entirely in images of sovereignty and language borrowed from an ancient oriental piety well acquainted with rulers who could do anything they wanted. God is the Lord, the Almighty, the King of the Universe, mover of people and nations, able to raise up and throw down those selected by divine and arbitrary choice, an imperial Presence with an ending in mind for the human experiment which cannot ultimately be altered. Like a shrewd monarch, God has tolerated disobedience from a forgetful subject people only so long before being "forced to lift the grace which lay upon their land, just enough to cause them to turn back to Him. A drought, or an epidemic of smallpox, or an Indian uprising would come, and the wisest of them would remember. . . ."[2] On the other hand, as children can sometimes wheedle and cajole a firm parent into occasional favors, "God has always responded just as men have prayed [,] . . . moving

God to do what He would not otherwise do if prayer were not offered." [3]

For the Christian Right, power is the reality which defines the relationship between God and humankind. All power is really in God's hands, despite appearances to the contrary. The only proper posture for God's people is submission to the divine will in obedience and humility. That is the posture God demands, and which is rewarded with blessings in abundance. When disaster comes, it can be interpreted as the result of overstepping what God permits; it can be averted through repentance and gestures indicating that the offender has recognized the error of breaking God's laws and promises never to do it again. The only secure way of living before God is by following the rules, never presuming to a position to which we are not entitled, and confidently expecting to be blessed in return. From this perspective, there are no accidents, only the effects of God's favor or disfavor.

Even God's mercy and forgiveness are seen as functions of divine power and are dependent upon obedience. God's goodness seems aimed not at "the just and the unjust," as Jesus put it, but rather at those who obey—or repent. Writing of abortion, Falwell warns: "If we expect God to honor and bless our nation, we must take a stand against abortion. I do want to say to those millions of mothers who have had abortions that God is a God of forgiveness. No one has to live under a terrible weight of guilt. . . . The blood of Jesus Christ, God's Son, cleanses us from sin." [4]

Faith itself is seen as a form of submission. "Only believe," goes the old gospel hymn, which is to say, "Only surrender your own efforts at reasoning about God and making sense of things through your insight and experience, and God will reward you with a faith which is not dependent on reason at all." Indeed, the truth we need to know about God lies entirely beyond our rational processes, which are only human and therefore untrustworthy. Furthermore, the pervasive dimension of sin means that even when we deceive ourselves into thinking that we are being rational or reflective, our minds will trick us into thinking what we want, rather than what God wants. Faced with such delusions and temptations, human beings are not capable of finding their own way towards God's truth—the truth that really matters. Hence knowledge itself, at least the really important knowledge about God and God's demands, can come only when we surrender our reason. Truth itself requires obedience.

Such a conception of the roles of God and human beings betrays an attitude on the part of those who have it which is profoundly uneasy with the concept of *freedom*. On one hand, this conception can be infinitely attractive, dangling the possibility, as it does, of making our own choices before our eyes. But at the same time, it is perceived as a temptation too great to be tested, because once free, we would probably choose to satisfy our most selfish and uncharitable desires at the expense of everyone else in the universe. No one spends more energy defending freedom than the Christian Right; and yet it is such a frightening gift that no one seems to be willing to accept it on its own terms. The implication is that if we were really free, we would doom ourselves.

What lies behind this fear of genuine freedom seems to be the assumption that power means *the freedom to do exactly what you want*. The Christian Right cannot believe in that possibility, so it chooses instead a way of living and believing which is based not on freedom before God but on absolute obedience.

One of the problems with defining the only way of life worth living in terms of obedience to God's laws is that it requires that we be absolutely certain of just what those demands are. The only way Christians could dare to submit themselves without reservation to such a God would be if that God had provided an infallible means of communication. This is, of course, the basis of the Christian Right's insistence on the inerrancy of the Bible. Such an absolutely trustworthy oracle is indispensable

if Christian living requires total submission. It would be unthinkable to try to live such a life if the demands were not
readily at hand. Hence the fundamentalist attitude to the Bible
is not just one among many of the articles of faith in their
theology. It is the *sine qua non,* the essential vehicle by which
God communicates what is expected of those who would be
faithful.

Inner spiritual experience such as guilt and forgiveness and a
sense of certainty serves the fundamentalist as a kind of secondary authority. It bears its own assurance because it is identified
not with one's own decision making but with the voice of God.
Many of the preachers of the New Right make authoritative
statements which they declare to be the clear will of God. Falwell himself has been chided because during the 1960s he argued against clergy involvement in politics, while by the mid-
1970s he was militantly engaged in the political arena. His 1965
sermon, "Ministers and Marchers," proclaimed: "[O]ur only
purpose on earth is to know Christ and to make Him known.
Believing the Bible as I do, I would find it impossible to stop
preaching the pure saving gospel of Jesus Christ, and begin doing
anything else—including fighting Communism, or participat-
ing in civil-rights reforms."[5] When challenged to explain this
unusual shift of "certainties," Falwell responds that "moral
Americans" finally became so alarmed about the declining state
of the country that they became aware of the necessity to save
it from itself.[6] Such reversals, however, seem to have no effect
on the fundamentalists' belief that God dictated the Bible verba-
tim to willing scribes and that it speaks in an inner way with
equal clarity to bolster faith and to give a trustworthy sense of
certainty.

The Christian Right's obsession with God's power is directly
related to its vision of the world. Nothing is more important to
its adherents than clarity about the appropriate or legitimate
exercise of power. Valuing yet fearing power, the Right is
therefore extremely anxious about its opposite, weakness or

powerlessness. Only power which is legitimated by its world view is tolerable. This includes God's own power, a necessary and perhaps even valuable limitation on personal freedom which would otherwise be uncontrollable. Social forms of power are legitimate when they appear to have behind them both the force of custom and the function of restraining an otherwise chaotic freedom. These include the power exercised within the family, and the power of the state. Within the family, disorder is averted by obedience to family structures which bear a surface relationship to a New Testament model of the family as well as preserving a remembered expression of American family life. In that model, the father exercises authority (power) as head of the family, caring for his wife, who in turn joins him in ruling over their children. The New Right is certain that this order is "natural" because it is God's own plan. Any alternative would bring unthinkable anarchy to the household and ultimately to society.

The power borne by the head of the household is similar, in its sphere, to the power given the state in God's plans, and serves a similar function: the maintenance of order by restraining untempered freedom. In such theology, the state has no other reason for being than to provide a social order within which the individual can exercise freedom bounded by rules to prevent an excess of liberty from harming others. As one theologian, not associated with the Moral Majority, sums up this view: "We take it for granted that individuals should be free to go to the ice cream parlor and choose. . . . However, we also assume that the state should prohibit individuals from going to the ice cream parlor and forcing the waiter at gun-point to serve up a dish of tutti-frutti." [7] That is what the Christian Right confidently expects would happen if freedom were not restrained by superior—and legitimate—power.

Since power is the ultimate value in such faith, it follows that enemies are also described in terms of power. God requires an adversary whose strength is worthy of battle. Just as medieval crusaders painted their adversaries in larger-than-life terms so that their cause would have cosmic importance, the Christian Right portrays those arrayed against them in the language of myth. The Soviet Union is not simply a vast, potentially aggressive industrialized country whose intentions sometimes threaten our own. It is described rather in bestial terms as a rapacious monster out to devour the rest of the world. That may or may not be an accurate description of the USSR, but it is safe to say that the New Right is uninterested in any rational evaluation of the relative strength of respective military capacity. A nation in competition with the United States can be met only with power. No other response or restraint is conceivable.

It is doubtful too if more than a handful of persons sympathetic to the New Right have any conception of the basic beliefs of Marxism as a philosophy or an economic system. It is enough that they see it challenging American power in the world. There is almost no interest in exploring the roots of the conflict, or alternative ways to react to it. Power responds only to power. This essentially mythological view of reality accounts for the Right's terror of totalitarianism as it is practiced in Communist countries, while remaining remarkably sanguine about right-wing dictatorships which may permit far less freedom. To the Right, such authoritarian measures are directed towards restraint of civil unrest, strikes, or antigovernment agitation; the implication seems to be that if citizens were behaving themselves as they ought (being obedient to the state), they would have no reason to fear. The *right* to dissent is of almost no importance.

The other enemies which haunt the New Right can also be identified in terms of their presumed relationship to power. Secular humanism is considered dangerous because it dares to assume that a nation's identity can be structured without reference to God. The Christian Right fears that sooner or later God's wrath at this act of defiance will make itself felt. The feminist movement is seen as a threat to the family, but its real challenge is to a particular configuration of power within the family. Homosexuals and feminists who contradict the universality of the family model for society also ultimately question this power structure and are therefore seen as profound threats to social order based on that power. This deep fear of disorder or anarchy is not surprising. The truth is, Christians on the Right, like so many of their ancestors, cannot really conceive of a world organized differently from the model they venerate. They live in terror lest that order be eroded and that in the subsequent chaos, their own place in the order of things would be even less secure. They cannot even imagine an order based on something other than power; they are convinced that only force can restrain freedom.

Yet freedom is so attractive and desirable that any limitations conceived as illegitimate are ruthlessly resisted. The feminist movement is not only a search for freedom for women which goes beyond traditional bounds; it is also a threat to the power traditionally enjoyed by men and which they have assumed to be natural and appropriate. In the same way, the state's intrusion into private affairs is considered illicit when it goes beyond the function of keeping order and deterring crime. In particular, government's efforts to alter social or economic patterns in the name of the public's welfare, or to regulate the free market place, are considered unwarranted intrusions into private freedom and intolerable limitation of the individual's power. Nor does the New Right look with favor on any efforts to redefine the structures of power and authority, whether from groups of Americans historically excluded from power (such as minorities), or from poor nations demanding a new economic order. The Right believes that order as it was once established in America enjoys the blessings of the God who is its author and whose power is the determining factor of all reality. Tampering with that order, they believe, will bring only disaster.

## The Right's Theology of Power

What can we make of such a point of view? We must begin from its fascination with, and even veneration of, power. As

God's primary characteristic, power defines the object of worship and ultimate value. The human condition is interpreted in terms of power; every act is evaluated as it enhances or controls power.

Such a theology betrays a primal fascination and awe about the exercise of power. Rudolf Otto describes the ultimate religious consciousness of God as the *mysterium tremendum et fascinans*—the awesome and fascinating mystery, at once infinitely attractive and fearsome. For the Christian Right, it is the power associated with God which both attracts and frightens. Freedom and power appear to be the same thing; hence freedom itself terrifies and excites.

If such theology is to be assumed as an authentic reflection on human life, then we must ask: What kind of experience could give us such a picture of God? What needs would be met by such a faith?

Theology which exalts power as the primary value and the basic truth about God belongs to people who have experienced power as the most desirable of goals. It is, in other words, the theology of people who perceive themselves as powerless or unfree, and therefore in need of power. What Hofstadter calls the "pseudo-conservatism" of the radical Right is, he says, "among other things a disorder in relation to authority, characterized by an inability to find other modes for human relationship than those of more or less complete domination or submission. The pseudo-conservative always imagines himself to be dominated and imposed upon because he feels that he is not dominant, and knows of no other way of interpreting his position. . . . [H]e has come to think of authority only as something that aims to manipulate and deprive him." [8]

Such people must have been so close to power that they see its many benefits, but have also suffered enough from its abuse to be aware of the need for restraint. They have noticed that the use of power appears to be arbitrary, and rarely benefits those who lack it. Even as it remains attractive and valuable, its underside is plainly visible. From this perspective, people see others apparently doing what they will. Jealous of their own small power, they long for more but instead confront their own weakness. The husband who is conscious on a daily basis of his vulnerability in most of the major areas of his life may well see the feminist movement as an attack on the one domain where he has power, as well as increasing his economic insecurity by encouraging women to enter the work force. His world may seem utterly beyond his control; he may have no opportunity for choosing where or how he works, and the fate of his neighborhood may be decided many miles away. The setting of his life is in other hands; but when he enters his home, he becomes master of the house. Women whose lives are even more at the mercy of structures and decisions beyond their control may be equally committed to a hierarchical family where at least they know where they stand. Even if their relationship to their husband is dependent, it communicates a form of safety found in few other spheres of life. The Equal Rights Amendment challenges the basis of the only security they know.

This model of reality poised on the boundary between power and powerlessness celebrates the quest for power through competition. Competing is the appropriate posture for the marketplace, in entertainment and sports, and even in the relationship with nature. The gun has assumed enormous symbolic value for the New Right as the instrument of power both in self-defense (the campaign to regulate firearms is interpreted as an attack on personal freedom) and as a means of struggling for power over nature (in the guise of animals). Hunting is often understood as a form of rite by which manhood is achieved, and it is the father's duty to teach the lore of guns and their use to his sons.

Nor should we overlook the element of power implicit in right-wing religion. Although the relationship with God is one of submission, at the same time the prayers of the properly humble get results. Christianity on the Right abounds with stories of businesses saved, misfortunes avoided, wealth procured, and success assured by attention to the divine commandments.

In his study of the politics and attitudes of the Right, Richard Hofstadter introduced the concept of "status politics" as "a product of the rootlessness and heterogeneity of American life, and above all, of its peculiar scramble for status and its peculiar search for identity." He claims that "in this country a person's status—that is, his relative place in the prestige hierarchy of his community—and his rudimentary sense of belonging to the community—that is, what we call his 'Americanism'—have been intimately joined. Because, as a people extremely democratic in our social institutions, we have had no clear, consistent, and recognizable system of status, our personal status problems have an unusual intensity."[9]

Some historians have attacked the concept as reductionist. Arthur Schlesinger, Jr. complained that "on close examination, the status approach appeared to adapt itself to every situation. . . . People moving up the social ladder, people moving sideways and people staying in the same place—all evidently suffered from status anxiety. . . . The status interpretation verges on becoming a heads-I-win-tails-you-lose proposition. It begins by explaining too much and ends by explaining all too little."[10]

But this criticism may in fact evade the truth behind Hofstadter's thesis, which is that the religion and politics of the Right flourish not as a function of material well-being but whenever people feel helpless to determine their own fate and alienated from those who appear to exercise power. It is precisely when they are most conscious of their vulnerability that people resent most any intrusion on the realms closest to them: the schools their children attend, their neighborhood, the ways they spend their money. Surely Hofstadter is correct in attributing this reaction to one's sense of identity and social worth within the complex fabric of society as a whole. How can people hold on to a sense of belonging when their jobs, their homes, their family life seem to be determined by others?

The heirs of populism are not interested in subtle distinctions among the trappings of status. Academicians and corporation heads may protest that they too are powerless; to the Right, they seem to share the tastes, attitudes, learning, and style of their rulers. All appear to be at ease with power. Meanwhile, the adherents of the New Right are acutely aware of how different are their own tastes and interests: they eat differently, speak differently, and dress differently. From such a perspective the world seems divided sharply between "us" and "them." "They" are the power brokers; "they" are the enemy, to be respected and envied, but also watched carefully and, perhaps, fought for control.

## A Theology of the Incarnation

Those Christians who do not and cannot conceive of humankind's relationship to God in terms of power and of the obedience to power find their theological base in what the church calls the doctrine of the Incarnation. Saint John's summary of the Incarnation—God's becoming flesh—is the starting point for what we can believe, not only about God, but about humankind in relation to God. It indicates that at least from the time of Christ, we are strangers no longer to one another. Indeed, in the light of the Incarnation, the whole of religious history can be read as the story of God's reaching out towards the human family in longing to be known. That yearning was fulfilled in the birth and life, the death and resurrection, of the man Jesus.

The Incarnation tells us something infinitely important about God, since it depicts God entirely in terms of a love so strong that it is willing even to participate in what we call the condition of being human. Everything else we believe about God must be seen in the light of that kind of love. This point should be noted, because Christians sometimes act as if love were simply one among many "traits" we assume about God. The Incarnation tells us that God *is* love; and that this love is directed in particular towards the human family, which owes its existence to God's mighty and creative Spirit and which is even described as bearing the very image and likeness of God.

That is why the Incarnation is also a theological statement about being human. It affirms, in the strongest possible way, the absolute value of humankind from God's point of view, even—and in spite of —the very obvious failings of every single member of the species when measured by the criterion of love which we identify with God. God's taking flesh is a cosmic act of faith in human beings, and represents God's own free choice to come to be with us in our frailty and our sin. Surely it is a measure of the value which Christian faith puts in the human that God is not ashamed to live out a human life, but rather willingly takes a place at our side.

The Incarnation is a great assertion of the value which being human has in God's eyes; it also indicates God's attitude towards the world. God has chosen to dwell in this world of flesh and blood. The man whose life is the life of God-in-the-flesh— the man Jesus—indicated time and again that we meet God here and now. Hence the doctrine of the Incarnation holds out a profound affirmation of the earth we call home. God has hopes for it.

The nature of that hope is revealed in the way God came to live among us. No commanding spectacle battered the world into obedience and fear; instead, a baby was born in Bethlehem. People sometimes wish for spectacle when they reflect on God's presence, because they would prefer certainty and clarity. Had God's arrival on the scene been announced with overwhelming fanfare, it would have carried with it its own authority. How could anyone resist or doubt such an unveiling? Perhaps the history of the world would have been very different if God had displayed mighty works in the sky. But we know that the coming of Christ was not that kind of event. Mighty acts there were, but they were often hidden, spoken of in back streets and alleys by people afraid to admit what they had seen. Those acts were not so much spectacles as they were *signs,* some as ordinary in appearance as breaking bread and naming it his body. Even Easter itself shows the presence of a Risen Christ easily misunderstood, not always recognized, never entirely convincing some of his friends.

Such behavior is not surprising, since God took flesh. To take on flesh means to assume the fullness of being human—even its shortcomings and ambiguities; its temptations, its appetites, its needs and pains; its limitations. Whatever else we can say about Christ, we must first say that he was a man.

To me, the great marvel of the Incarnation is that God chooses to be revealed in weakness. Saint Paul noticed it: Talking about Christ as a crucial part of God's revelation makes God look foolish and impotent. How absurd that the Word by which the Universe came into being should stand enfleshed and condemned by an arrogant and vain Roman functionary! How ridiculous that the source of life should die on a cross! It flies in the face of every ordinary grasp of divinity. No God of power and might as those words are ordinarily used could stand for such indignity. And yet so the story goes.[11]

Nor should it surprise us, since God is love; because the power of God *is* God's love. It is love's nature to make itself vulnerable, reaching out in the hope of a free response, not as a tyrant of the universe in search of cringing obedience.

God's taking flesh on our behalf is the chief sign of that love. It means that God reaches us primarily in the *human,* as the people who came to know Jesus saw for themselves. That is why loving God and loving your neighbor are two sides of the same coin. It is not that they are similar. They are the same phenomenon: As you have done it to one of the least, *you have done it to me.*[12] The Incarnation points us to our brothers and sisters in the human family as the meeting point at which we will find God, still veiled by all the frailty of the human flesh, but surely there.

## Power and Biblical Theology

The Bible's theology *is* about power; in that fact the Christian Right is correct. God took flesh in a world too brutal to bother hiding power from its agents or its victims. The Roman Empire, the greatest power on earth at the time of Christ, punished its challengers ruthlessly. But God was already familiar with such power. Many centuries before, God had called a people out of slavery in Egypt, where the iron hand of Pharaoh had kept them in bitter submission.

In the face of such power, the Bible is a nearly unbroken hymn to freedom: freedom from oppression, freedom from injustice, freedom from sin, freedom from death.

The story of creation lays the foundations for the Bible's declaration of freedom. God's gift to the man and the woman is the freedom to choose. They are placed in charge of the garden, and entrusted with *naming* what they find: They share in the work of ordering the whole creation. Even when they disobey and discover the way things are—that separation from God and death always go together—God does not destroy their freedom. The story of the human family's life with God is told in terms of that monumental gift on God's part: God trusts us with the creation. Its fate is, indeed, in our hands. Its future is open; God waits and watches to see whether we will live up to our possibility and nurture it or instead will choose foolishly and bring it all down with a hideous crash. The place of humankind within nature and at home in the universe is defined by the freedom God gives us. It is power over ourselves; it is power over our destiny. God is truly "the One who lets us be." God stands back to give us room to be ourselves, like a wise and loving parent who knows that until we have space to choose, we will be incompletely mature. Christ himself never battered down his enemies or grasped at power to effect his will. To the contrary, he invited willing followers, not cringing and submissive servants. Some of his harshest words were reserved for those who imposed their will on others. We know too that while he spoke out fearlessly against oppression, he chose silence and death rather than limiting the freedom of those who chose to kill him—surely the supreme example of "letting be." Martin Marty points out that "the Christian faith calls people to be, before it calls them to be good. To be means for them to find themselves grounded in the care of God, transformed by the love of Christ, whole. To be good calls them to serve as channels through which that love reaches others."[13]

Such freedom in human hands witnesses to God's act of faith and affirmation towards the human race. Knowing the ease with which we fall, God nevertheless hands us the power we need to choose our future.

Of all the biblical writers, it was Paul who explored this theme most fully. In writing to the Christians in Corinth, he marvels that God has chosen the way of freedom even though it implies a certain weakness on God's part. After all, giving freedom to us humans and coming to dwell among us as a man involved God in the run-of-the-mill world we all inhabit; but more than that, it put God at our disposal. *We could do what we wanted with God.* That is why Paul had to wrestle with Jewish scorn and cultivated Greek disdain: What kind of God would allow such treatment by mere creatures? Paul knew the answer: a God whose power lies not in sheer strength of arm but in the power of love. Love includes an element of vulnerability and weakness, even of suffering. Some Christians are offended by the possibility that God might be in pain, because they prefer the image of power and might. But love is inconceivable without pain. Paul's point is that the weakness God accepts by loving the world is really a kind of strength far greater than mere power.

Furthermore, the Bible assures us that God is less interested in servile obedience than in the freely given response of love ("We love because God first loved us")[14] and that true obedience is directed towards the human family. The insight of the prophets as they probed more deeply into the heart of God was just that: worship means nothing apart from attention to the needs of the human community.

> What are your endless sacrifices to me? says the Lord. I am sick of holocausts of rams and the fat of calves. The blood of bulls and goats revolts me. . . . I cannot endure festival and solemnity. Your New Moons and your pilgrimages I hate with all my soul. They lie heavy on me, I am tired of bearing them. . . . Cease to do evil, learn to do good. Search for justice, help the oppressed, be just to the orphan, plead for the widow.[15]

The prophet Micah summed up God's demands in this way: "This is what God asks of you: only this, to act justly, to love tenderly, to walk humbly with your God."[16] Obedience to God is expressed in our behavior towards others.

God's love towards the human family carries with it God's affirmation of human value, expressed on the human level in the concept of *covenant*—the bond between God and humankind and also between people. All relationships among us take place within that common bond we share as God's children. Paul also clearly understood that within that community, meant ultimately to include us all, *laws cannot ultimately serve to determine the life of faith.* From Paul's point of view, our relationship with God can never be summed up in sheer obedience but rather by choosing to love. The search for a Christian way of life is not a matter of following timeless laws. It is rather the search, undertaken in freedom, for ways of being and living which respect the human family (including our own dignity) and which are appropriate to express our awareness that Christ offers us freely given love. The limits of our freedom are not those of law but of our care for others—our covenant with them.

The Bible is the story of how some people have tried to live faithfully by being attentive to what they glimpse and hear of God, and how a people dedicated to that life have fallen and risen and never finally surrendered their faith—nor did God surrender faith in them. The Bible is a remarkable collection of such stories, but because it belongs to the times in which it was written, it betrays the many points of view, and the shortcomings, of its authors. To claim an eternal and absolute value for everything it contains is to miss the whole point of what it is and is not. Consider: The Bible cannot be essential to Christian faith, since we know for a fact that the New Testament was in formation for many years after Christ. Even allowing for the most radically hasty composition of its books (which flies in the face of authentic scholarship), there must have been a whole generation or more of Christians who never saw the New Testament as we know it. We know too that what we call fundamentalism is *not* the "old-time religion." To the contrary, Christians in almost every age have recognized the errors of fact, the development of ideas which sometimes contradict thoughts that came before, and the symbolic (we might say mythological) nature of some of the biblical material. As notable an early Christian as Augustine, who could hardly be called a "liberal" theologian, was converted to Christianity at the turn of the fifth century. In his spiritual autobiography, the *Confessions,* he mentions that when he first read the Bible he was horrified to imagine that Christians could be expected to believe everything he found there. He was so put off that his conversion depended upon his discovery that the Christians of his day were accustomed to reading the Bible critically, interpreting allegorically the material which they knew could not be true. Christians in most ages have understood that the Bible is not "magic" in the sense that its authors received dictation from God. They wrote out of the deep conviction that what they had to say was true, and very often, especially when it had to do with their life with God, it was. But truth is not abstract, coming down from heaven by pipeline, any more than God's presence has ever come among us in such a way. Why, if God was subjected to the flesh and the world of Jesus, should we expect God's Word to be somehow splashed across the pages without any of the ambiguities of humanity? If Christ shared such ambiguities and limitations, surely God's Word in written form must be subject to the same finitude. The Bible is a document for all seasons, but it is also *historical,* which means that it belongs to its times and those who wrote it. It seems to me a special kind of religious egocentrism to assume that comments which seem to apply to events spread over many centuries should in fact turn out to address only our own. Yet the preachers of the Right seem obsessed with finding hidden clues to our own history in books that deal with ancient world events and empires dead for three thousand years.

Fascination with interpreting biblical prophecies as if they applied to the present or the future is one of the recurring aspects of fundamentalist religion. Biblical scholars can usually identify for us the ancient figures and events which the prophets were addressing; but populist preachers have preferred to see their messages as signs of the imminent arrival of Christ in their own times. The fact that nineteenth-century preachers were proven wrong has not deterred their successors from the same message.

Pat Robertson, of the Christian Broadcasting Network's "700 Club," offers to subscribers willing to pledge at least fifteen dollars monthly his key to "the Bible's earthshaking prophecies." The Bible, he assures us, "contains specific references to coming world events, all of which point to the Second Coming of Jesus Christ and His reign on earth. We can use these prophetic messages of Scripture as a guide in following the course of world events." What Robertson has in mind is "the Last Days, Russia's invasion of Israel, the antichrist, increase of earthquakes and volcanoes, the Second Coming of Jesus Christ." [17]

Hal Lindsey, author of *The Late Great Planet Earth* and *The 1980s: Countdown to Armageddon,* explains why prophecy can be trusted in our time when earlier generations were misled. The answer, he tells us, "is simple. The prophets told us that the rebirth of Israel—no other event—would be the sign that the countdown had begun. Since that rebirth, the rest of the prophecies have begun to be fulfilled quite rapidly. For this reason I am convinced that we are now in the unique time so clearly and precisely forecast by the Hebrew prophets."[18] Never mind that Israel was restored in 538 B.C. Lindsey ignores that piece of information because he wants to be able to predict *our* future.

So, it would seem, do many other people. Lindsey claims some thirty million readers. Nearly a quarter of a million subscribers to the "700 Club" receive a regular bulletin called *Pat Robertson's Perspective,* which not only reveals the Bible's secrets but also gives concrete advice for avoiding the painful side of the Last Days. Robertson warns of another "downward lurch" in the world's economy, hyperinflation, and final collapse. Allowing for "God's specific instructions to you" as well as a warning to note personal circumstances, earnings, taxes, and "special knowledge," Robertson suggests using resources to "build God's Kingdom and help others"—and invest in government securities. He also recommends survival skills and supplies, avoiding savings accounts, and looks favorably on the purchase of gold and grain.[19]

This "fundamentalism of the future" betrays an insecurity about what is to come as certainly as fundamentalism of the past and present reflects anxiety for security now. If the future does not lie in human hands but, to the contrary, has been predetermined by an omniscient and all-powerful God, then all we must do to be safe is to learn how to plumb the mysterious volumes in which it is foretold. Anyone who can do so is an object of veneration. Surely fifteen dollars a month is not too much to pay for answers to what lies ahead and, even more importantly, how we may protect ourselves.

Although that search for certainty has tempted people throughout the church's history, it denies the God-given gift to share in building the future. If God has already decided its end, history is a sham. Such a divine agenda makes a mockery of human freedom and the choices of people and nations don't really matter.

Most Christians in most ages have assumed that the Bible must be read with the eyes of reason as well as faith, and in company with those who share the life of which it speaks.

The search for truth—and this includes the truth about God and the Bible—is an honorable and humane undertaking, worthy of us among whom Christ was not ashamed to live and who are also God's children. God affirms a freedom which would be useless without the gift of reason which is part of our nature. If the twentieth century has shown us the limitations of that reason and the surprising role of our emotions in what we thought was "only" rational, that is no excuse to abandon reason but only to beware of trusting it too far. God stands by us when we fall into error; otherwise, why would we be created free? God's Word can stand up to the scrutiny of those who seek to understand its origins as well as its end. The God who submitted to the frailty of the flesh would surely not object when we peer closely at the record of our ancestors to study the nature of their life with God.

The absolute power which the Christian Right attributes to God betrays a deep and human longing for freedom. God wills us to be free, not to do whatever we will, but to take responsibility for ourselves within the human community to which we are eternally bound. The power we possess is the power to love as God loved us—love which *lets others be* and affirms them in all the dignity of the image of God. When we move towards that love, we are already living with one foot in the City of God.

# The Nation Under God

> "We need leaders of moral courage
> today who know that there is safety
> only in strength, not in weakness."
> —*Jerry Falwell*[1]

> "All who live by the sword shall
> die by the sword."
> —*Matthew 26:53*

The Christian Right's ambiguity about power is nowhere more evident than in its attitude towards America. As God's chosen instrument among the nations, the United States is called to be the invincible bastion of freedom in a threatening world, always eager to press the battle against its enemies; at home, its government is to be equally resolute in protecting its citizens against the subversive dangers which lurk everywhere. Yet it must never use that mighty power to its own ends or to further the welfare of its people; the slightest gesture of activity beyond what might be called the "police function" crosses the invisible boundary of private freedom and becomes tyranny.

The Moral Majority cannot conceive of meeting power with any response except more power ("Russians understand only force").[2] It has therefore been an ardent and vocal advocate of increased military and defense spending in the face of what Falwell calls a no-win policy on the part of American leaders due to their "lack of nerve to confront the spread of communism."[3]

The result, he complains, is that "ten years ago we could have destroyed much of the population of the Soviet Union had we desired to fire our missiles. The sad fact is that today the Soviet Union would kill 135 to 160 million Americans, and the United States would kill only 3 to 5 percent of the Soviets. . . . From 1971 to 1978 the Soviets outspent the United States by $104 billion for defense and an additional $40 billion for research."[4]

Books such as Claire Sterling's *The Terror Network*[5] inflame the New Right's fears by claiming to document a chain of subversion that traces almost all political unrest to Russian ploys. Ernest LeFever's *Amsterdam to Nairobi: The World Council of Churches and the Third World*[6] complements Sterling's work by interpreting the World Council's support for African and other independence movements as witting or unwitting support for international Communism on the part of the WCC's staff. Such publications ignore the complex relationship among right-wing oppression, disregard for human rights, and South African *apartheid,* considering them irrelevant in the face of the Communist monolith. The New Right seems incapable of conceiving of any cause or motivation for world events other than Communism; it is the focal point around which the maelstrom of international events revolves.

The aggressive, even interventionist posture demanded by the Christian Right in international affairs stands in curious contrast to its ideology of domestic politics, where the least government is the best government and power is to be used only in deterring crime. One of the clearest statements of the theory which the Moral Majority unites to its ideology is William E. Simon's *A Time for Truth,* a celebration of American free enterprise as the economic intention of its founders and the system which defines American identity. Simon, who headed the Oil Policy Committee in the Nixon administration and served as President Ford's secretary of the Treasury, describes himself as competitive and uninterested in academics as a young man. Like the populists of every age, he disdains what he considers the "irrelevance" of intellectuals: "I felt some remorse over my undistinguished academic record until, decades later, I discovered that the American intelligentsia vastly preferred impecunious Ph. D.s who destroyed the economy to successful but Ph. D-less financiers who fought to save the economy, at which point I got some inkling of why the academic world had failed to inspire me. My remorse vanished."[7]

In Simon's view: "America was born a capitalist nation, was created a capitalist nation by the intent of its founders and the Constitution, and developed a culture and a civilization that were capitalist to the core. But this capitalist, or free enterprise, identity is true of no other nation. . . . An American who is hostile to individualism, to the work ethic, to free enterprise, . . . is in some profound sense advocating that America cease being America."[8] In fact, he goes on, such a person "is striking out against the most fundamental unifying principle of our society. Historically the 'Americanization' of the immigrants to our shores has followed their voluntary acceptance of the capitalist culture, its economic modes and its ethics. An ethnic, racial, and religious 'melting pot' was able to turn into a unique and new culture, precisely because that 'melting' required the unification of all around the Horatio Alger ethic and the free enterprise system."[9]

What Simon and his supporters in the Christian Right affirm is the classical economic theory known as *laissez-faire,* an unregulated economy in which the "single most awe-inspiring thing about our economic system" is "the fact that the flood of wealth emerges from the lack of state-imposed or 'national' purposes and goals. The capitalist miracle occurred in the United States, the politically freest nation in the world, precisely because this explosion of wealth is uniquely a result of *individual liberty.*"[10]

Several things should be noted about this defense of classical capitalism. First, it reflects the New Right's attitude about power: Our national greatness, which requires the most belligerent attitude towards power among the nations, also requires *absolute political freedom*—i.e., absolute private power—on the individual level.

Second, this theory rests on the belief that economics is itself a private matter, based, in Simon's words, on "the most individualistic and the most democratic economic system conceivable. It works with no conscious direction. . . . There are literally billions of purposes, billions of decisions, billions of adjustments every day as inventors, entrepreneurs, middlemen, employers, workers, buyers and sellers pursue their own respective self-interests. . . . This is the system that has endowed the average American with the highest standard of living in the world and in history—even if the job of eliminating the last pocket of poverty is not yet completed."[11]

It should also be noted that this system is commended to us because it *works*—a pragmatic rather than a moral judgment, although Falwell is convinced that "the free-enterprise system is clearly outlined in the Book of Proverbs."[12] Furthermore, Simon and his Christian supporters believe that economic free-enterprise is *inherent* in American identity, and therefore a part of the divine givenness of this country and its culture. To describe an economic system, a functional structure, as a matter of identity betrays a commitment based not on reason but unexamined ideology.

All such ideology rests ultimately on that act of faith in the chosenness of America. The national identity conceived as vocation, both as an example to the world and as a special relationship with God which brings its own special blessing, underlies all the Christian Right's speculation about what it means to be an American. Because of its image of God and its experience of power, it attributes the obvious spectacle of American might as evidence of its nearness to God. But it fears any signs of decline in that supremacy, by whatever standard it is measured, as evidence of God's disfavor or a shying away from our vocation as a religious and moral nation.

It is this fascination with morality as both the sign and the condition of God's blessing that leads the Christian Right to fear so much the evidence of growing tolerance or "permissiveness" in American society. Because this tendency is so dangerous to a religious understanding of American identity, it is associated in the mind of the New Right with an external enemy: The continued decline in traditional moral standards will, says Falwell, so weaken the structure of American society that "there would be nothing to hold this country together. Communism could easily take over."[13] It is for this reason that Christians allied with the New Right have taken to the political arena in increasing numbers. Their targets are signs not so much of political as of moral subversion: abortion, secularism in the educational system, and permissiveness in the media.

The New Right's objection to abortion stems from the belief that human life begins at conception, that all life is a gift from God, and that murder is forbidden by the Ten Commandments. What makes it more than a private matter is that the United States Supreme Court removed restrictions from abortion in 1973; hence, in Falwell's words, "America has the blood of all those babies on her hands."[14] In fact, "no one person or state has the right to decide whether another human being should be allowed to live."[15] America's fate at God's hands depends upon how we as a nation act in ending the slaughter of innocent victims.

Since it denies that it is a private moral issue, the Christian Right has sought legislation to prohibit abortion. A proposed constitutional amendment—the so-called Human Life Amendment—would make abortion a federal crime except in cases of rape, incest, or endangerment of the mother's life. In 1981, a "human life bill" was also introduced into Congress which would define human life as "deemed to exist from conception." Organizations such as the Planned Parenthood Federation and the National Organization of Women charge that the campaign to limit abortion by legislation threatens the whole spectrum of family planning. "More is at stake," read one appeal from Planned

Parenthood, "than the fundamental right to decide whether and when to have children. At stake is whether a vociferous minority group has the right to impose its moral views on anyone else."[16]

## Education, Freedom, and the Christian Right

When William Jennings Bryan died shortly after prosecuting John Scopes for teaching the theory of evolution in a Tennessee classroom, most Americans believed that an era had ended. They supposed that public educational institutions had won the right to promulgate current scientific thinking without fear of attack from religious opponents. Fifty years later, that has proven to be untrue. As the media expose large audiences to fundamentalist preaching and create militant networks of activists, many states have been challenged by parents drawn from the ranks of the Christian Right to give "equal time" to an alternative theory of the creation of the world. They call this viewpoint "scientific creationism." Most seem prepared to interpret the time frame of Genesis symbolically, and to accept that the earth may be as old as natural science tells us. What they demand is that creation not be taught as an autonomous or undirected process without reference to a Creator God, and that schools teach seriously the possibility that human beings were created independently—"special creation"—rather than descended from nonhuman ancestors.

In a 1981 court case, Kelly Segraves, father of three school children, sued the California Board of Education, charging that the board's 1978 teaching guideline which describes evolutionary theory as "the only credible theory of the origin of . . . life" violates his family's freedom of religion. Segraves's suit was supported by the Creation-Science Research Center, a parents' group dedicated for nearly twenty years to "correcting the philosophical imbalance regarding evolution and creationism issues in public education."[17]

The judge did not uphold Segraves's case since in fact the

challenged guidelines direct that evolution be taught only as a "conditional statement."[18] "Creationists" were pleased, however, because the court also ordered the Board of Education to emphasize the provisional nature of instruction about evolution.

Both Arkansas and Louisiana have recently enacted legislation requiring that evolution and scientific creationism be taught as equally sanctioned options. State Senator Bill Keith, sponsor of the Louisiana legislation, commented, "The Genesis account explains what happened. Scientific creationism, through scientific data, explains how it happened."[19]

In an effort to raise public awareness about the issue, Falwell's organization placed an advertisement in several mass-circulation magazines which read:

> Cast your vote for creation or evolution. Where do you stand in this vital debate? 1. Do you agree with the "theories" of evolution that DENY the Biblical account of creation? 2. Do you agree that public school teachers should be permitted to teach our children *as fact* that they decended from APES? 3. Do you agree with the evolutionists who are attempting to PREVENT the Biblical account of creation from also being taught in public schools?[20]

Respondents were urged to mark their choices and return the "ballot" to Falwell's organization.

In general, the attack on evolution proceeds on two fronts. The first is that some of the early assumptions made by scientists proved to be wrong or even deceptions. The other is the doctrine of biblical inerrancy. Scientific creationism is not, by definition, scientific, because it does not rest its conclusions on the evidence of free inquiry. Its bounds and conclusions are predetermined; it is orthodoxy, not science. Isaac Asimov argues that if court cases demanding the teaching of "creationism" succeed, "we will have established the full groundwork . . . for legally enforced ignorance and for totalitarian thought control."[21] "With creationism in the saddle, American science will wither. We will raise a generation of ignoramuses ill-equipped to run the industry of tomorrow, much less to generate the new advances of the day after tomorrow. We will inevitably recede into the backwater of civilization and those nations that retain open scientific thought will take over the leadership of the world and the cutting edge of human advancement." [22]

One does not have to agree with Asimov's prophecy to realize that the Moral Majority's effort to impose religious limitations on the teaching of science betrays deep anxiety. It seems to fear the search for truth, lest articles of unexamined faith be challenged. The society it seeks is not based on reason; it is imaged from assumptions that may be neither examined nor questioned.

Mel and Norma Gabler, of Longview, Texas, head an organization known as Educational Research Analysis, dedicated to monitoring and challenging textbooks used in public schools. In his book *Listen, America!* Jerry Falwell devotes an entire section of his chapter on "Education" to an approving review of their work.

The Gablers and their allies in the New Right watch for textbooks and literature which might be critical of American traditions and which seek to understand, rather than evaluate, human behavior. Perhaps it is this unwillingness to make moral judgments about types of behavior condemned by fundamentalist Christians that most upsets the Right. Says Falwell: "Until about thirty years ago, the public schools in America were providing . . . support for our boys and girls. Christian education and the precepts of the Bible still permeated the curriculum of public schools. . . . Our public schools are now permeated with humanism." [23] The result is that "children are taught that there are no absolute rights or absolute wrongs and that the traditional home is only one alternative." [24] As Norma Gabler asks: "Why shouldn't we fight? It's our children, our tax money, and our government. And it's our rights that are being violated. If textbooks can't teach Christian principles, then they shouldn't teach against Christianity." [25]

Like other critics on the Right, the Gablers' organization

claims that many textbooks "undermine patriotism, the free enterprise system, and parental authority; that the books are 'negative' in their discussions of death, divorce, and suicide; that the books erode absolute values by asking questions to which they offer no firm answers." [26]

The National Coalition Against Censorship reported in March, 1981, that no fewer than five states and the District of Columbia had cases pending in which films or books had been attacked on moral grounds. Recent cases have challenged best-selling works such as Eldridge Cleaver's autobiography, *Soul on Ice;* Joseph Heller's novel *Catch-22,* and Anthony Burgess's *A Clockwork Orange;* Langston Hughes's anthology, *Best Short Stories by Negro Writers;* books such as *Our Bodies, Ourselves;* and many other well-known works, both fiction and nonfiction. [27]

Still another area of Christian Right activism is its campaign to force removal of television programming which it considers morally objectionable. The Coalition for Better Television, chaired by the Reverend Donald Wildmon with Falwell's support, announced a plan in 1981 to organize a national consumer boycott of companies which sponsor "permissive" programming. The coalition had in mind programs which portray divorce, extramarital sex, and homosexuality as morally acceptable, depict unnecessary violence, or criticize the United States too freely. Wildmon claims that in 1977–79, "90 percent of all sex on TV was outside of marriage," and that "during an average year of prime-time viewing, the TV audience is exposed to 11,531 sexually suggestive comments or scenes of implied sexual intercourse." [28] However, shortly before the national boycott was to begin, its leadership announced that it was being canceled in view of the networks' apparent willingness to monitor their programming with more care. Some suspected, however, that opposition from anti-Christian Right organizations such as People for the American Way and indications that fewer than half the Moral Majority's own membership supported censorship may have contributed to the decision.

The aggressive posture by the New Right following its election victories in 1978 and 1980 has increased its willingness to repress domestic opposition to its political goals. In 1981, the United States Senate established a Judiciary Subcommittee on Security and Terrorism chaired by right-wing Senator Jeremiah Denton of Alabama, who was elected with Moral Majority support. The Heritage Foundation, a think tank founded by noted New Right figures Paul Weyrich and Joseph Coors, supported the formation of the subcommittee and recommended that it investigate not only Communist party activity in the United States but also "clergymen, students, businessmen, entertainers, labor officials, journalists and government workers [who] may engage in subversive activities without being fully aware of the extent, purposes, or control of their activities."[29]

## Interpreting the New Right's America

Writing as long ago as 1954, Richard Hofstadter noted the appeal of what he called "pseudo-conservative" politics:

> For two hundred years and more, various conditions of American development—the process of settling the continent, the continuous establishment of new status patterns in new areas, the arrival of continuous waves of new immigrants, each pushing the preceding waves upward in the ethnic hierarchy—made it possible to satisfy a remarkably large part of the extravagant status aspirations that were aroused. There was a sort of automatic built-in status elevator in the American social edifice. Today that elevator no longer operates automatically, or at least no longer operates in the same way.[30]

He considered that Americans have a peculiarly urgent need to *prove* that they "belong." When anxiety about declining opportunities to do so is combined with other factors, especially fundamentalist fear of Communism, the necessary ingredients are present to allow for an irrational and extreme patriotism interpreted in religious terms.

The truth is, the Christian Right's attitudes towards the state reflect its ambiguity towards power in general. In particular, its adamant intention to use political power to enforce its moral judgments contradicts its own insistence that absolute economic freedom is God's intended order of things. On one hand, it extols the virtue of *laissez-faire* as the God-given "natural law" of economics. But it admits too that the media have enormous power to manipulate desires into "needs" and then make a profit by meeting those needs.

Its attitude also flies in the face of traditional American attitudes to individual freedom. For example, Thomas Jefferson wrote: "I am really mortified that . . . a book can become a subject of inquiry, and of criminal inquiry, too. . . . Are we to have a censor whose imprimatur shall say what books may be sold and what we may buy? . . . Whose foot is to be the measure to which ours are all to be cut or stretched?"[31] Indeed, a consistent libertarian would argue for the decriminalization of pornography and abortion on the grounds that if that is what people want, that is what they should be free to have.

The American Civil Liberties Union, historically a guardian of the libertarian position, considers that the patriotism of groups like the Moral Majority "violates every principle of liberty that underlies the American system of government. It is intolerant. It stands against the First Amendment guarantees of freedom of expression and separation of church and state. It threatens academic freedom. And it denies to whole groups of people the equal protection of the laws. . . . In fact, the new evangelicals are a radical anti-Bill-of-Rights movement. They seek not to preserve traditional American values, but to overthrow them."[32]

The Christian Right clearly suffers from inconsistency about its economic and political principles. If in fact it believes that people should control the economy through their private choices, then those choices must be permitted. If, on the other hand, the welfare of society demands that certain kinds of choices be forbidden, then the state has assumed the power to intervene—as the Moral Majority demands that it do with respect to "moral" issues. The Christian Right cannot have it both ways. Its calls for censorship fly directly in the face of its own economic and political principles. Nothing could contradict more completely the principle of *laissez-faire* than efforts to legislate private matters of morality.

The ideological nature of the Right's commitment to those principles can also be seen in its unwillingness or inability to question whether changed historical circumstances might render their theories obsolete or in need of revision. Many economic historians note that *laissez-faire* economics came into favor at a time when commerce largely involved small businesses, independent farms, crafts, and trades. Free-market economics expects that wealth will be dispersed so that all will compete on more or less equal terms. If that competition is limited by the concentration of capital, economic freedom becomes illusory and the power of a few will be able to control the entire system. Many believe that the process of industrialization during the nineteenth century had precisely this effect. Mass production and the accumulation of capital drove small independent enterprises out of business. Everyone knows that the corner grocery cannot really compete with the giant supermarket chain. In fact, uncontrolled economics in the last century created not only great wealth and periods of prosperity but also sweatshops, child labor, and a working force often at the edge of starvation. *Laissez-faire* economics operates on the very principle which the New Right professes to hate: Darwin's "survival of the fittest." Could it not be argued that this system is too cruel to be allowed to function without safeguards lest it produce not prosperity but greater and greater inequality?

In the period since the Second World War, capital has been passing into what has come to be called the "multinational corporation." These institutions can be seen as limitations on economic freedom because they further limit competition, and hold considerable power in their own hands. Many have become anxious that such corporations can play off American workers against cheaper labor in other countries, and in recent years plant closings have eliminated thousands of American jobs. In many cases the companies which close their own plants reinvest their capital overseas in order to increase their profits, but without any regard for those whose jobs are destroyed by the decision.

The other side of this process, rapid and uncontrolled importation of industry into underdeveloped countries, has been criticized for destroying the traditional culture and social fabric, polarizing rich and poor, and creating inhuman slums when cities grow too rapidly. This underside of the free-enterprise system when it ignores human consequences challenges the principles of the New Right in ways of which it seems unaware. Simon's secure faith that the "last pocket of poverty" will soon be eliminated cannot be based on reason. The truth is, the lower level of the economic ladder is getting poorer, not richer, and not only overseas but in the United States as well. In 1980, the United States Census Bureau reported that 13 percent of the American population—nearly one in eight Americans, or more than twenty-nine million people—had incomes below the poverty level, compared with 11.7 percent just one year earlier.

Richard Viguerie does criticize what he calls "big business" because of its alliance with "big government." "It is not true that what is good for General Motors is good for the country—or that what is good for big business is automatically good for conservatives. . . . Big Business is comfortable with red tape, regulations, bureaucracy—these things freeze the status quo, impede newcomers, and hold down competition."[33] What he fails to question is how "big business" got that way—and whether, given present realities, the old ideology would work the way he expects.

## Politics and Biblical Theology

While claiming to rest on both traditional American and Biblical principles, the New Right's assumptions about the state in fact distort both history and the authentic perspective of the Bible.

The scriptures present two very different images of the nation: one of them based on the experience of Israel, the other grounded in the first Christians' experience of living under a hostile Roman Empire.

The nation of Israel understood itself as a theocratic people, that is, ruled ultimately by God. This rule was exercised at first through charismatic tribal leaders who emerged in times of crisis (the Judges) and later through a monarchy which was understood as God-given (although an alternative tradition considered the Kings a negative addition to national life, opposed by God, and conceded only reluctantly).

Because it held an essentially religious conception of itself as a covenant community, Israel always considered itself to be related to God not as a collection of individuals but as a *people.* God's covenant was with Israel, not Iraelites; it was a corporate rather than individualistic sense of identity. The primary value within this covenant-community, required by God's own commandment, was *justice.* Justice defines the appropriate behavior for every member of the nation-community of Israel towards every other member.

The concept of justice is elaborated through the Hebrew scriptures, but always contains a minimum standard of behavior towards others within that community. At the very least, justice means giving all others the right to live in peace. This is the basis for the prohibition against murder found in the Ten Commandments, which, it must be remembered, were intended originally only to regulate behavior within the covenant-community. Moses also delivered to the people God's prohibition against dishonoring parents and ancestry, stealing from one another, lying, taking another's wife or other property, or even envying another's blessings. These are considered to be the principles on which life in the covenant-community can exist and flourish, and imply that each individual son of Israel (the commandments are directed towards the male members of the community) gives to his fellow Israelites the right to prosperity and peace. The Hebrew word *shalom,* "peace," is a much richer and more positive concept than the English implies. It includes not only the absence of violence but food and drink in plenty, harmony with the creation, and in general those conditions which are necessary to an abundant life with God in the unity of the covenant-community. This image of the perfectly just community not only served as the criterion for judging every society in history, including that of Israel itself, but also helped form the content of the hope for the City of God which fed the prophets' dreams.

It will be seen that this concept of justice includes the right to live in freedom, in the sense that each son of Israel is meant to enjoy this justice equally. But it is by no means an image of absolute social freedom. Rather, the freedom of each is limited by the demands of justice. Freedom, for example, does not include the right to profit from the misfortune of others. Such freedom is limited in several ways, such as prohibition of interest when loaning money to a needy person, and by the remarkable institution of the Jubilee year described in the Book of Leviticus whereby twice each century all property gained is to be returned to its original owner. Whether or not this custom was actually observed, it signals the Bible's insistence that justice places bounds on economic freedom. Furthermore, the prophets in particular argued that membership in the covenant-community demanded that freedom be tempered by compassion towards the needy. Some of the most violent condemnations recorded in the scriptures are directed towards those who have added to the misery of others for their own economic gain. Consider these passages in the light of what they imply about uncontrolled economic freedom:

> Woe to the legislators of infamous laws, to those who issue tyrannical decrees, who refuse justice to the unfortunate and cheat the poor among my people of their rights, who make widows their prey and rob the orphan.
> (Isaiah 10:1–4)

> All are greedy for profit and chase after bribes. They show no
> justice to the orphan, the cause of the widow is never heard.
> (Isaiah 1:23)

Perhaps none spelled out more clearly than the prophet Amos
the biblical viewpoint on justice:

> For the three crimes, the four crimes of Israel I have made my
> decree and will not relent: because they have sold the virtuous
> for silver and the poor for a pair of shoes.
> (Amos 2:6)

> Listen to this, you who trample on the needy and try to suppress
> the poor people of the country, you who say, "When will New
> Moon be over so that we can sell our corn, and sabbath, so that
> we can market our wheat? Then, by lowering the bushel, raising
> the shekel, by swindling and tampering with the scales, we can
> buy up the poor for money, and the needy for a pair of sandals,
> and get a price even for the sweepings of the wheat."
> (Amos 8:4–6)

Even the Psalms, the hymns of Israel, reiterate the same theme:

> Happy the one who cares for the poor and the weak:
> if disaster strikes, the Lord will come to help.
> The Lord will guard that person,
> give life and happiness in the land.
> (Psalm 41:1–2)

God's blessing depends not upon one's attitude towards power
but towards weakness.

Throughout the long and complex history of the Hebrew people, they were never permitted to forget that from their God's
point of view, the demands of righteousness were fulfilled by
how they behaved towards those most in need. It should be
noted that in their attacks on the corruption of the rich, the
prophets were not simply condemning criminal activity; nor were
they urging the rich to charity. Rather, their point was that

justice is fulfilled in the care of those who are most needy. The poor are *entitled* to what they need by virtue of being part of the covenant-community. No social goal is more important for biblical religion than the attention given to the poorest of the poor, the least among the people, and those helpless to care for themselves (especially, in a time when families provided the only security, those who were without families—widows and orphans).

The New Testament expands the idea of the covenant-community beyond the people of Israel to include all those who have been redeemed by Christ—which is to say, the whole human family. It is Jesus' contribution to biblical ethics that he came to see all people as encompassed by the covenant of God with the whole creation, and therefore entitled to the requirements of justice by virtue of being the children of God.

From the biblical perspective, undeterred pursuit of riches is judged to be "proud" and therefore contrary to the covenant. The Psalms in particular laugh at the arrogance of those who make the pursuit of profit their chief goal. Whatever the level of their honesty, the Bible tends to see them as foolish.

This was the viewpoint of Jesus himself, who argued that the whole point of the Law—the summary of obligations laid upon us by our covenant with God—is to serve those in need. He also shared the Psalmists' perspective that wealth is an unworthy and ultimately rather silly motive: one of his starkest parables concerns someone who keeps amassing wealth, only to die in the night. "You fool!" says Jesus, speaking on God's behalf.[34] His well-known comment about the relative ease with which camels pass through a needle's eye and the rich find their way to God's City is also noteworthy: from the biblical viewpoint, wealth is unworthy of human effort and a distraction from what really matters.[35] The state's interest in power, enormous as it was in Jesus' time, is equally trivial in his eyes: hence his remark to give Caesar what is his; we have more important things to concern us.[36] God's will, as Jesus continually assured us, is that all our needs be fulfilled from a nature rich in its universally intended gifts.

This nearly unbroken biblical point of view provides Christians with critical theological principles by which we can evaluate any political and social order. The primary value must be justice, defined as providing adequately for the needs of all people, and caring especially for those unable to defend themselves against greed and power. Perhaps another way of expressing the Bible's imperative is that no one's plenty should be at the expense of another person's need. Christians who are serious about judging society by the biblical standard must always ask themselves: Does the political and economic order allow for all people's needs to be met with the dignity to which their humanity entitles them? This principle can be applied to communities, to the life of a nation, and with respect to relationships among nations. Because the biblical concept of justice demands respect and harmony among people, no society deserves to be considered just unless it gives to every person the full share of dignity demanded by the image of God. From this perspective, let us turn to some pressing questions which are raised by the concerns of the Christian Right.

*The Dignity of Human Life.* Many Christians agree that respect for human life extends to the unborn fetus. The Moral Majority, however, seems to take a cavalier attitude towards life *after* birth. For example, its fascination with the balance of terror between the United States and the Soviet Union puts it in the position of resisting efforts like the Strategic Arms Limitation Treaty controlling nuclear weapons and advocating instead a posture fraught with the possibility of mutual destruction. For the foreseeable future, the choice is between an international effort to bring the development and deployment of weapons of terror under control and ultimately to reduce them, or a constant increase in arms based not on reasonable defense but on irrational fear and love of power for its own sake. We might well ask whether Falwell's concern about our ability to destroy a "mere" ten million Russian people is consonant with respect for human life and dedication to *shalom.*

In 1981, the Primates who head the churches of the Anglican Communion noted that "the Church in former ages justified war in certain circumstances by recourse to the theory of the 'just war'." This theory, they observed, "was never intended to commend war, but to limit its frequency. There have always been Christians who repudiated any legitimizing of war. Today, many others would join them, believing that the very conditions required for a just war themselves condemn not only the actual use of nuclear weapons, but also their possession as a deterrent." While doubting if such a position would commend itself to the whole church, the Primates nevertheless insisted that they were not "indifferent or uncommitted." "We pledge ourselves to work for multilateral disarmament, and to support those who seek by education and other means, to influence those people and agencies who shape nuclear policy. In particular we believe that the SALT talks must be resumed and pursued with determination."[37]

*How We Spend Our Money.* In 1980, writes Episcopal priest George Regas, world expenditures for weapons reached $490 billion. That, he says, "is madness. It is a criminal, sinful mismanagement of the earth's resources. It is unfaithful stewardship. $490 billion on arms and 2.5 billion of God's people go without any professional health care. . . . 1.5 billion of God's people have no safe drinking water. . . . 1 billion of God's people live in absolute poverty, that is, a state of almost constant malnutrition."[38] Ironically, just when human services are being curtailed in an effort to control American inflation, the Governing Board of the National Council of Churches warns of a "turn from America's search for peace through negotiation in order to seek it through military predominance"[39]—the most inflationary monetary policy of all. A truly biblical theology must ask the Christian Right, Do Jesus' words about how we behave towards enemies justify meeting power with more power?

Would the New Right's image of America and the priorities which follow it enhance the well-being of *all* our people? What about racial minorities who suffer a legacy of oppression? The elderly? Those who live in regions where unemployment approaches 50 percent? The young? The veterans whose minds, bodies, or spirits were permanently crippled by the last war? Does the New Right's vision of America unleashed bring *them* protection, well-being, and hope? If it does not, then the Bible's standard and demand for justice are unfulfilled.

*The United States among the Nations.* A truly critical, biblically based theology will also lead us to ask ourselves hard questions about the effects of American behavior on other peoples. Many Americans seem to believe that our self-understanding as God's chosen people gives us the right to act without being subject to such evaluation. But a critical theology means that we must always ask such questions.

For example, one of the New Right's early issues was the treaty returning control of the Panama Canal to Panama (or as the Right described it, "giving away" "our" canal). The issue from their perspective allowed for no discussion. In Ronald Reagan's words, "The Canal is ours. We built it. We paid for it. And we intend to keep it." [40] The issue of justice was not raised. It was assumed that the United States would do what was best not only for itself but for Panama, in the traditional style of the great power "supervising" its client. It was, however, precisely the issue of justice which led to passage of the treaty over vehement New Right opposition. Secretary of State Henry Kissinger admitted that "the 1903 treaty (which spelled out the American possession of the canal) is not viewed anywhere in the world as equitable and just. We wouldn't stand a similar arrangement in our country." [41] Discussing his own decision to support the treaty returning control of the canal to Panama, former senator Thomas J. McIntyre wrote, "After six months of hard study, I have concluded that on balance the new treaties are the surest means of keeping the canal open, neutral and accessible to our use—and are *in keeping with our historical commitment to deal fairly and justly with lesser powers.*" [42]

We might also examine critically the New Right's reading of international affairs with regard to what Falwell calls "that miracle called Israel." [43] The Christian Right's position on Israel is somewhat contorted. On one hand, its fundamentalist reading of the New Testament persuades its advocates that the Jews will ultimately be damned if they do not accept Jesus as Messiah. On the other hand, so many of the biblical prophecies seem to focus on the future of Israel that they cannot afford to ignore it. The restoration of Israel in 1948 is not only interpreted as the key to those prophecies, but also, in Falwell's view, a sign of God's faithfulness and blessing. "The Jews are returning to their land of unbelief. They are spiritually blind and desperately in need of their Messiah and Savior. Yet they are God's people, and in the world today Bible-believing Christians in America are the best friends the nation of Israel has. We must remain so." [44]

Clearly the New Right's support of Israel is based neither on respect for its people, nor on an obligation to assist a nation whose existence is threatened, nor on a reasoned or critical reading of the international situation. It rests rather on a fundamentalist interpretation of biblical passages which addressed conflicts nearly three thousand years old but have been misunderstood to concern modern Israel, the Arabs, and the Russians. This nonrational political motivation betrays a patronizing arrogance towards the peoples and religions of the Middle East.

Given its own ambiguity towards power, ought we not examine more closely the New Right's fascination with American power among the nations? Is the exercise of American political and economic power always—or customarily—in the service of an international order based on justice? Is that power ever misused to our own honor and glory at the expense of lesser nations—perhaps even the equivalent of those helpless for whom

God seems to show such concern? Do we really place our enormous resources at the service of justice? Why, then, was the United States in 1981 the only industrial nation to oppose international supervision of the sale of baby formula, in the face of well-known studies indicating its devastating effects in poor countries? Do such actions celebrate the cause of God's justice—or an idolatrous worship of power? Does continued American support for South Africa as a bastion of anti-Communism serve the biblical cause of justice in the light of that country's cruel racial policies? Or is it based on considerations of power only? What about our policies towards dictatorships of the Right which protect our country's economic interests? Did the decades of support for Somoza in Nicaragua benefit that nation's poor—or the corporations which relied on Nicaraguan labor, products, and materials? Has American policy toward El Salvador been based on our care for the poorest of the poor as the Bible commands, or does it stem from fear of Communism? Is American support for Israel, the heirs of Nazi holocaust, joined with attention to the suffering of the Arab people which an authentic faithfulness to biblical principles demands, or is the New Right's interest solely in countering Arab militants and in a fundamentalism which denigrates Judaism and the Jewish people? Have we as a nation been faithful to God's priorities as the Bible makes them clear, or to an ideology which reads the Bible from the misconceptions of power?

And is it really appropriate to consider ourselves the Chosen People and the successor among the nations of God's Promised Land? Honoring the deep experience of liberation and salvation which the settlers felt upon arriving on these shores, is it really fitting for us their descendants to continue to act and believe as if we were somehow special and unique? Is it not more a sign of that pride which the Bible considers a temptation? Does the biblical story of God's call to Israel not rather demonstrate that God acts first on behalf of the weak and humble among the nations of the earth? Does our self-image protect us from the kind of rational and critical self-examination enjoined upon us by our biblical faith? Mark Hatfield, senator from Oregon and well known for his Christian commitment, has written:

> Believing that our nation has a special dispensation of God's blessing as opposed, for instance, to Norway or Tanzania or Yugoslavia, simply confuses any biblical understanding of God's relationship to our nation and the world. God is not choosing special peoples over others in the modern world. . . . Nevertheless, the Old Testament can still teach us about God's standards of justice for any people and any nation, and the accountability of earthly powers to these exacting standards. In this way, the Old Testament does have a direct and poignant relevance to the Christian's relationship toward America, or any modern secular state.[45]

Every Christian can agree with the New Right that we are called to struggle for a political and economic order, an American nation among the nations of the world, which is faithful to the biblical vision. But it is a long way from the ideology of the Moral Majority and its uncritical proclamation of an imaginary past to the vision of the City of God. God's demands will never be realized until the worship of power gives way to the Bible's principle of justice. In Senator Hatfield's words:

> The Christian is committed to molding his or her life to Christ's. We are to seek his power and follow his style of leadership. This means washing one another's feet, laying down one's life for his friends, and loving one's enemies. The politician who follows Christ is in no way exempted from obeying 'all that has been commanded'. He or she is called to be a servant-leader. Self-preservation is no longer the key motive in all political activities; rather, it becomes the service of human need, and prophetic faithfulness to a vision of God's will being done 'on earth as it is in heaven'.[46]

# The Home Front

"People today need an anchor.
My husband is committed to an America
where that anchor—religious faith—
is not being cast out the window."
—*Mrs. Jerry Falwell* [1]

"God Almighty created men and women
biologically different and with
differing needs and roles."
—*Jerry Falwell* [2]

"Marriage can be preserved only if
we allow family structure to change."
—*Carolyn G. Heilbrun* [3]

The family functions for the New Right as America in microcosm. As the state is the institution given by God for the ordering of national life, so the family is the institution which gives order and meaning to the individual in society. It is a social structure created by God, and therefore enjoys the potential not only for God's blessing but also the opportunity to fulfill a divine mission. It is to control the unruly affections of a sinful human race whose passions would otherwise lead them into moral and social anarchy; it is the institution responsible for passing on from generation to generation the unsullied religion of the Bible; and it is called to hand down the values and traditions of America. Parents have the primary obligation for their children's moral, ethical, and spiritual training, and because this duty was given them by God, it can be abandoned only with extreme consequences. Just as the mission of America is a sign of divine favor but also carries the threat of punishment for failure, so the family is an institution of great promise but labors under the possibility of judgment. The fate of America is in the hands of its families: as Falwell warns, "No nation has ever been stronger than the families within her."[4]

When Falwell speaks of the family, he means "the marriage of one man and woman together for a lifetime with their biological or adopted children."[5] As the "fundamental building block and the basic unit of our society,"[6] the family is presumably for everyone; certainly the Moral Majority makes no provisions for those who, by choice or accident, find themselves outside such a family unit.

The family as the Christian Right portrays it is a nuclear group organized hierarchically with the man at the head, exercising spiritual leadership and also caring for the material well-being of his wife and children. Although subordinate to her husband, the wife shares in the training and discipline of their offspring.

In support of their assertion that this model of the family is God-given, Falwell and others cite several well-known passages from the New Testament, notably Paul's discussion of the proper relationship between husband and wife in his letter to the Ephesians, and the reference in 1 Peter to women as "the weaker sex."[7] It seems to the Christian Right that this biblical image has been fulfilled in the traditional American family: dependent upon the father for strong leadership, firm discipline, and financial support, and looking to the mother to serve as "homemaker" and to dispense tenderness as a gentle counterpart to the father's stern hand. In such a household, children grow up to understand the proper character of manhood and womanhood. Men are to be strong, unmoved, independent, and responsible; women are sensitive and emotional, fragile and dependent, but are also able to understand their call to temper their husband's strength with gentle feminine mercy.

Falwell insists that such a family does not degrade women; to the contrary, "because a woman is weaker does not mean that she is less important." [8] Although they may have greater needs than men, "in families and in nations where the Bible is believed and practiced . . . women receive more than equal rights." [9] The roles of the sexes are "designated by God. God's plan is for men to be manly and spiritual in all areas of Christian leadership. . . . Women are to be feminine and manifest the ornament of a meek and quiet spirit. . . . In the Christian home the woman is to be submissive. . . ." [10] Nor do women belong in the work force; their children need them at home.

Falwell finds support for this view in the work of Dr. Harold Voth, senior psychologist and psychoanalyst at the Menninger Foundation, who considers mothering to be "the most important function on earth. . . . A woman needs a good man by her side so she will not be distracted and depleted, thus making it possible for her to provide rich humanness to her babies and children. Her needs must be met by the man, and above all she must be made secure. A good man brings out the best in a woman, who can then do her best for the children. Similarly, a good woman brings out the best in a man, who can then do his best for his wife and children. Children bring out the best in their parents." [11] In Falwell's opinion, those who decline to accept those roles live "in disobedience to God's laws. . . ." [12]

## Challenging the Image

Because the family is so fundamental to its world view, the Christian Right perceives no greater danger than the threats which challenge it: changes in traditional sex roles; homosexuality; divorce and extramarital sex which imply that sexual relations are not confined to permanent marriage; and the erosion of parental authority over children.

Falwell considers the chief impetus for modifying the traditional sex roles to be what he calls the "feminist revolution," [13] led by "women who were once bored with life, whose real problems are spiritual problems. Many women have never accepted their God-given roles." [14] That revolution is focused in the campaign for the Equal Rights Amendment, which Falwell labels "a delusion" [15] and "a definite violation of holy scripture," [16] since women need and deserve more than equal rights if they are to survive and prosper. Its error, and its threat, lie in the fact that it challenges the divine norms for defining what is feminine (and masculine). In addition to its disastrous effect on women, Falwell warns that the women's movement will affect the family in three other ways: It will weaken men; by removing children from the influence of their mother, it will contribute to increasing governmental control over the young; and it will lead to a rise in homosexuality by blurring and confusing sex roles.

Homsexuality, in Falwell's mind, is "Satan's diabolical attack upon the family, God's order in Creation." [17] While expressing pastoral care for gay people since "Jesus Christ loves every man and woman, including homosexuals and lesbians," and is even able to "forgive and cleanse people guilty of this terrible sin," Christians should not confuse loving and helping them with acceptance of "their perversion as something normal." [18] Falwell is convinced that homosexuality is not an innate tendency but learned behavior: "A person is not born with preference to the same sex, but he is introduced to the homosexual experience and cultivates a homosexual urge. It is innocent children and young people who are victimized and who become addicts to sexual perversion." [19] Failure to stem the increasing acceptance of homosexuality as an alternative life-style to marriage will, in his words, "not only have a corrupting influence upon our next generation, but it will also bring down the wrath of God upon America." [20]

Underlying all the New Right's anxieties about the future of the family is its faith that the institution of marriage is undergirded by absolute values, coupled with its perception that those values are being denied or ignored by powerful forces within American culture. If Communism is the chief threat to America on the world scene, its domestic handmaiden is the secular humanism which contradicts the Right's understanding of the American past and its ideals. Every American institution has suffered from humanism; Moral Majority-backed Senators Orrin Hatch and Jeremiah Denton claim that the United States government has an ideology about sexual behavior which is spread by "family planning" clinics and which teaches that "teen-agers' sexual activity is inevitable and acceptable so long as no pregnancy results; contraceptives should be made available to teen-agers at Government expense; if unwanted pregnancy does occur . . . abortion is the only logical alternative." [21]

Nowhere does the threat touch children more seriously than in the public school system. The importance of the schools lies in the fact that they shape and, to some extent, control what children think and believe, and therefore can overrule the influence even of parents whose fundamentalist faith is impeccable. (This was the underlying anxiety which led fifty years ago to the Scopes trial.) The New Right uses all possible means to call the attention of the American public to the danger of this menace. *Let Their Eyes Be Opened* is a documentary film which has circulated widely among Christian schools, parents' groups, and fundamentalist churches. It features textbook critics Mel and Norma Gabler among others and sets out to explain "what humanism is, how it is antithetical to Judeo-Christian principles, and how it is influencing school curricula and young people's behavior. Humanism is shown as a root cause of the modern-day breakdown of educational effectiveness, discipline and morals, and also as a possible prelude to what some would like to see as a new world order, devoid of moral absolutes and restraints of the past." [22]

Writing in the New Right *Christian Courier,* Bette Norman asserts that the "values taught at school ARE NOT the same as those taught by the majority of American parents. The laws are no longer upheld; to the contrary, children are given a broad spectrum of values and told to make up their own value system!"[23]

For increasing numbers of Christians on the Right, the answer is an alternative educational system, the "Christian school," in which carefully selected teachers inculcate fundamentalist religion, "traditional" values, and science free of the taint of evolution. Norman considers that "the ONLY solution for Christian parents is to remove their children from (public schools) and place them in a Christian atmosphere which WILL teach the same value system as that being instilled at home."[24] The rapidity with which "Christian" schools have been established across the United States (at a rate of several a day) is one of the most obvious and potentially far-reaching of the effects of the New Right on American social and institutional life. (On the other hand, for parents whose time with their children is limited and for whom a "Christian" school is not a possibility, there are other resources: the "Home Health Education Service" offers "amazing results in two months" to parents who follow its program, "The Bible Story," "to mold your child's character the pleasant way. . . . The secret is that THE BIBLE STORY was not written just to tell the wonderful stories in the Bible, but each story was especially written to teach your child a different character-building lesson—lessons like *honesty, respect for parents, obedience, cost of stubbornness,* and many more."[25]

Early efforts by the New Right to defend its image of the family from the onslaught of humanism centered on defeat of the Equal Rights Amendment and of civil rights legislation for homosexuals, and limitation of abortion. The extent to which it intends to utilize the legislative process in support of its beliefs became clear in 1980, when Nevada's Senator Paul Laxalt introduced a Family Protection Act into the United States Senate. Reintroduced in substantially the same form by Senator Roger Jepsen of Iowa, elected with the support of the Christian Right, in the following year, the act contained a potpourri of measures designed to strengthen the federal government's support for the family as the New Right conceives it. These included prohibiting the use of legal-services funds for cases which involve homosexual rights, abortion, or divorce; an annual tax exemption for families whose children attend private schools; restoration of voluntary prayer in public school classrooms; and permission for children to be excused from classes "teaching the functions of becoming a parent."[26] In the same year, a bill affirming "traditional values" was introduced into the California legislature which would require that the state board of education "adopt instructional materials that convey such things as the importance of the family unit; the principles of free market economy, including the role of the entrepreneur and labor; the importance of respecting the law and the universal values of right and wrong." Commenting on the legislation, Cal Thomas, Moral Majority reporter, observed, "Such values used to be taken for granted. Now we have to pass laws in order for our children to hear about the great principles that established and built America."[27]

## The Ideology of Sex and a Critical Eye

It should come as no surprise that the Christian Right's image of the family rests not on a historical perspective or a critical reading of the scriptures but represents rather the personal side of its ideology of power. The Moral Majority and the women's movement agree on one point: the issue at stake is indeed power, power and weakness experienced within the context of marriage and the American family. The New Right claims that the relationship between the sexes in which the husband holds power on behalf of his weaker and more vulnerable wife is supported by an appeal to American tradition and also to the Bible.

Historians tell us, however, that the family structure as the New Right envisions it is in fact a relatively recent development, which came into its own only with the advent of the

Industrial Revolution and the urbanization of America. In the early days of this country, work was carried on primarily in the home, on the family farm, or in small business or craft enterprises which were located in or near the family living quarters. This was the context for work which Thomas Jefferson considered to be the dominant, and appropriate, means of livelihood for Americans, and it is the form on which the theory of *laissez-faire* economics was built. In such a setting, women were an integral, and necessary, part of the work force. The family depended for its survival upon the wife's constant and productive labor, whether in the home or in the fields.

> She was an artisan as she spun and wove cloth from wool, flax or cotton, and then made clothing for her family. She knew how to preserve vegetables, meat, and fruits as well as make candles or soap. She may have been an herbalist or a midwife. Depending upon where she lived, she may also have taken care of livestock, worked in the fields, or hunted and trapped. Though she was likely to bear a child every two years for twenty years, the upbringing of the children was not solely her responsibility. Mothers trained daughters and fathers trained sons into the interlocking household where all essential goods were produced. No household member worked for a wage.[28]

Alice Kessler-Harris's work reminds us that the model of the family as preached by the Christian Right stems from the division of labor which took place when men began leaving the home in large numbers to earn their livelihood. This radical social change of a century ago redefined work to mean "work for which wages are paid," while the labor of women shifted from "coproduction" to that of maintaining and sustaining the household. Among middle-class Americans of the nineteenth century, the image of women as homemakers and guardians of family morality became an ideal, both for themselves and for those families striving for upward mobility and "respectability." Survival on a husband's income became a sign of affluence, and the ability to maintain his family on his earnings alone was a test of masculine responsibility. "Since women 'belonged' in the home, those who worked were relegated to unskilled and low paying jobs on the theory that they were preparing for married life or supplementing a husband's income."[29] One side effect of this model of the family was to overlook or undervalue the work of women in the home. As Kessler-Harris comments: "To describe women's household work as merely auxiliary to paid work in the labor force, or to talk about some women as 'not working' ignores both the value of housework in sustaining the labor force and its relationship to the wage working lives of women. Wage work and household work are two sides of the same coin."[30]

The family as the New Right describes it is *not* the "traditional" model of the American family. It is a model related to a particular time in history and one social class, and accepts that middle-class ideal as the absolute standard of respectability and propriety. It is in fact only one among many possible models of family life, and the New Right's insistence on its validity is related to the pervasive ambiguity about power which colors its ideology. The middle-class image of the family in the form in which the New Right describes it provides a setting where both men and women can be certain about power. For men who experience powerlessness in most of the areas of their life, such a model of the family creates an island where they are in control. Yet even its most ardent defenders sometimes seem uncertain whether their image is actually based on the reality of the nature of men and women or on concerns about status and power. Consider these words of Richard Viguerie: "Our family was thrifty. No money was ever wasted. My mother worked in a paper mill during World War II, doing a man's work. I suspect she actually did the work of several men."[31] Describing the beginning of his career, he writes: "It was particularly hard for my wife, Elaine, in our early years. She not only took care of our two small children, but she handled most of all the duties normally handled by the husband, such as repairs to the house and car, yard work, paying bills, etc. This allowed me to spend as many as four hours a day studying direct mail in addition to holding down a full time job." [32] Both Viguerie and other New Right leaders such as Jerry Falwell applaud the work of Phyllis Schlafly, who chairs the national Stop the ERA movement. She is, in Viguerie's words, "also president of Eagle Forum, a national organization of conservative women, author of nine books, syndicated columnist, former CBS radio commentator, wife and mother of six children, an attorney, a debater without equal— the heart and soul of a woman's movement which believes in family, God and country." [33]

It is difficult indeed to reconcile these testimonies to the energies and stamina of women with the New Right's ideology that they are weak and must be sheltered in the home. We can find a hint of impropriety about a woman "doing a man's work" in Viguerie's comments, but certainly no evidence for his ideology. The values the New Right affirms are the product of convention and status anxieties rather than any ultimate truth about women and men.

Some scholars argue that in fact, the model of the family which emerged in the nineteenth century and which the Moral Majority defends with such vigor has had disastrous consequences for both men and women. Carolyn Heilbrun suggests that asserting that men are stronger than women forces men to deny their vulnerability and allows women to exercise their will only through secret manipulation. Such dependence denies women an authentic identity of their own. One female opponent of the Equal Rights Amendment remarked, "I don't care to be a person," [34] prompting Heilbrun to observe that in traditionally structured families, "to be a person and a wife are oddly incompatible." [35] The truth about humankind is that "we are all of us, men and women, complex, superior one moment, frail and helpless the next." [36] By denying this fact, the male-dominated family produces "men incapable of loving, and women incapable of selfhood." [37]

Indeed, Heilbrun argues that the image of the family espoused by the New Right is in fact *responsible* for the widespread breakdown of the family because it is built upon a false understanding of the nature of men and women. She is convinced that an authentic relationship between the sexes depends upon the very intimacy and vulnerability to one another which male dominance denies.

> Marriage is now failing before our eyes, but its preservation depends upon the restructuring of the family, where 'strength' and 'weakness', 'fragility' and 'endurance' are not assigned by gender. The irony here, as in all essentially reactionary positions, is that those most interested in preserving the family in its nineteenth century form are, in that very act, destroying its cornerstone, marriage. . . . Our present family structure produces children incapable of the very heterosexual love it has tried to inculcate. In insisting upon 'mothering' as the function only of one female figure, we have made impossible the companionship of men and women.[38]

> It should by now be clear that the old family structure is not only crumbling, but where it persists, it is, in fact, making *more* likely the very conditions that the defenders of conventional family life most deplore: homosexuality, divorce, and casual sex. . . .[39]

The Christian Right replies to critiques like Heilbrun's by arguing that its model of the family is based on scriptural norms. Paul's letter to the Ephesians directs:

> Wives, be subject to your husbands, as to the Lord. For the husband is the head of the wife as Christ is the head of the church, his body, and is himself its savior. As the church is subject to Christ, so let wives also be subject in everything to their husbands. Husbands, love your wives, as Christ loved the church and gave himself up for her. . . . Even so husbands should love their wives as their own bodies. He who loves his wife loves himself. . . . Children, obey your parents in the Lord, for this is right. 'Honor your father and mother' (this is the first commandment with a promise), 'that it may be well with you

and that you may live long on the earth'. Fathers, do not pro-
voke your children to anger, but bring them up in the discipline
and instruction of the Lord.[40]

1 Peter is equally firm:

> You wives, be submissive to your husbands, so that some, though
> they do not obey the word, may be won without a word by the
> behavior of their wives, when they see your reverent and chaste
> behavior. Let not yours be the outward adorning with braiding
> of hair, decoration of gold, and wearing of robes, but let it be
> the hidden person of the heart with the imperishable jewel of a
> gentle and quiet spirit, which in God's sight is very precious.
> So once the holy women who hoped in God used to adorn them-
> selves and were submissive to their husbands, as Sarah obeyed
> Abraham, calling him lord. And you are now her children if
> you do right and let nothing terrify you. Likewise, you hus-
> bands, live considerately with your wives, bestowing honor on
> the woman as the weaker sex, since you are joint heirs of the
> grace of life, in order that your prayers may not be hindered.[41]

Certainly the burden of proof is upon those of us who would
argue that such advice should not be taken as the last Christian
word in the relationship between the sexes. However, if we are
to take a genuinely critical approach to the ideology of the
Christian Right, we must measure not only historical traditions
but even specific biblical texts against the overall teaching of
the scriptures *as a whole.* If we undertake to do so, we will, I
believe, discover that in fact there is no single biblical ideal or
teaching about marriage. Rather, we will find that there is a
whole spectrum of prohibited and prescribed behavior between
the sexes which changes radically over the centuries and which
owes its institutional forms not to a specifically biblical point
of view but to the culture in which biblical religion was being
practiced.

Marriage in the early stages of Hebrew religion was not so
much a private matter between husband and wife as a legal

covenant between families. The Bible is nearly silent on the subject of sexual relationships between unmarried people; the Song of Solomon, which contains some of the most sublime poetry in the Old Testament, is an erotic love song between two unmarried lovers. The commandment against adultery is concerned not with the sanctity of marriage but with protecting a man's property. Wives were bought and sold like all other property, and a man's prosperity could be measured by the number of wives. Their function was primarily to ensure the survival of the family by producing sons, and marriage by no means prevented a man from keeping one or more concubines for personal pleasure, companionship, or family survival. We find such a marriage in the story of Abraham and Sarah, ancestors of Israel: when Sarah is unable to produce a son for Abraham, she offers him her Egyptian maid in the hope that their liaison might be more fruitful. Their grandson Jacob worked for seven years to purchase Rachel from his uncle Laban, but Laban tricked Jacob into marrying her sister instead. Rachel's purchase price was another seven years of labor, at the end of which Jacob found himself in possession of both sisters, one of whom he loved, the other disdained. He also received a maid from Rachel when she became alarmed that she was barren. The Book of Numbers quotes Moses' command, presumably spoken in God's name, that after the conquest of Midian the Israelite men are to kill all the adults but to save the young girls for themselves.

Such marriage practices persisted throughout much of Israel's history. It is true that the small army of wives and concubines possessed by the kings occasionally troubled the prophets, but what they feared was the intrusion of foreign princesses into Israelite society. They were disturbed not by the *number* of royal spouses but by the possible contamination of Israel's religion by alien cults.

It can be safely assumed that when the Moral Majority speaks of defending the biblical ideal of marriage, the Old Testament's model is not what they have in mind.

By Jesus' time, the custom of multiple wives had died out, but marriages remained the basic institution of society and the accepted norm of human behavior. As in earlier periods, producing "sons of the covenant" remained both a duty and a sacred privilege. Women received their status and identity through their family, first through their relationship to their father and then to their husband. Only marriage and the family provided women with a secure place in society. The plight of the widow with no family to support her was pitiable indeed (see, e.g., the Book of Ruth). It was for this reason that the custom of *levirate marriage* survived for many centuries: When a woman was widowed, it was the duty of her husband's brother to take her into his household lest she starve to death. For the same reason, divorce was a terrible fate for a woman, who was then left without any means of support except her own family. We might well interpret Jesus' hostility to divorce primarily in terms of his concern for the plight of its victim. Jesus' insistence that a man who has divorced his wife and married another is committing adultery is a notably profeminist position: the Jewish Law was originally concerned not with affront to a wife but with protection of a man's property.

Another hint of the tenuous position of widows in the society of the first century survives in the reminder in 1 Timothy that widows who have no families are the responsibility of the congregation.[42]

In spite of these indications that marriage is part of the accepted world we live in, it must also be said that for the New Testament, marriage is by no means an absolute. Neither Jesus nor Paul considered the family to be as important as the Reign of God for which they were preparing. Jesus himself, to the best of our knowledge, was never married, and his relationship to his own family seems to have been less than ultimate. On one occasion, when his friends reported that his mother and brothers were looking for him, Jesus replied, "Here are my mother and my brothers! Whoever does the will of God is my brother, and sister, and mother."[43] Nor did Jesus have any hesitation in calling his disciples to abandon their families and follow him. It should be remembered that part of the challenge of his call to them was the necessity of leaving behind their wives and children. "Whosoever loves father or mother more than me is not worthy of me."[44] To a potential follower who asked for time to bury his father, Jesus spoke even more harshly: "Leave the dead to bury their own dead; but as for you, go and proclaim the kingdom of God."[45]

This somewhat casual attitude towards the family makes sense only against the apocalyptic background of the New Testament. Its authors believed that in Jesus, God's Reign had begun and would soon arrive in all its fullness, bringing the justice and *shalom* for which they had been waiting. At that time, every human institution would pass away; all would be made new. That belief seems to have colored Jesus' actions and expectations. His challenges to the social order were concrete and specific; he attacked neither the empire, nor slavery, nor the prevailing customs and mores of his time, except when they clearly violated God's demand for justice. There was neither the means nor the need to make a revolution; everything was about to be transformed.

In his behavior towards women, however, Jesus did contradict the social norms of his own day and culture by assuring them of their dignity and worth and their place in the City of God. Many of his encounters make the point. We have already noted, for example, the attention to the well-being of women in his teaching about divorce. His conversation with a Samaritan woman shocked her as much as his friends; drinking from her vessel as he did violated the ritual law in favor of a gesture of respect and compassion. Jesus' friendship with Mary and Martha and his willingness to talk religion with them demonstrates an attitude of sexual equality unknown in his generation. Perhaps most importantly, he appeared to a group of women on Easter morning even before the Twelve saw him, although women were considered too unreliable to serve as witnesses in Jewish courts. Surely the point is that the Risen Christ trusted himself to their testimony even if his contemporaries did not.

The widely held assumption that they were living in the last days lies behind the social conservatism of the New Testament writers. Neither Paul nor the authors who followed him were interested in radically restructuring society to meet the demands of faith. Books like 1 Peter seemed concerned that Christians draw as little attention as possible to themselves, living quietly in confidence that very soon this world would be transformed into the eternal City of God. In the meantime, they were to behave, as far as possible, as if they were *already* citizens of God's City. The church provides them with a foretaste of what is to come.

Paul himself shared in the judgment that marriage was unimportant in view of the imminent arrival of the Reign of God. He himself never married, and seems to have considered marriage as a distraction from the work of proclaiming the Gospel. He suggested to the Christians in Corinth that it would be better to abstain from sexual relations altogether, but realized that others had more trouble than he in controlling their passions. Marriage is preferable to promiscuity (or in Paul's pithy words, "It is better to marry than to burn").[46] Dealing with a situation which may never have faced Jesus, he even suggested that a non-Christian spouse could be divorced, although he thought it preferable that the marriage continue. When he troubles to spell out his theology, he insists that living as if we were already in the City of God radically changes the demands placed upon us. This is spelled out most clearly in the letter to the Galatians: "There is neither Jew nor Greek, there is neither slave nor free, there is neither male nor female; for you are all one in Christ Jesus."[47] The letter to the Christians in Galatia is a hymn in praise of the freedom into which Christ has called us. Among Christians, power has no place in any human relationship. It has been transformed by the demand for justice and mutual love.

What are we to make of this remarkable spectrum of ideas and visions of marriage and human sexuality? Perhaps the New Testament scholar Walter Wink is correct when he writes that in fact *"there is no Biblical sex ethic.* The Bible knows only a love ethic, which is constantly being brought to bear on whatever sexual mores are dominant in any given country, or culture, or period."[48] The same Book of Leviticus which prescribes death for homosexual behavior also decrees exile for a married couple who have intercourse during menstruation. The mores of the Old Testament are the product of ancient taboos connected with sexuality which far antedate Israelite religion; reactions to the customs of the people they feared; and the forms of marriage and social relationships which prevailed in the Middle East during the time of its writing. New Testament attitudes towards marriage reflect the custom of its time and the apocalyptic expectations of its writers, for whom human relationships of any kind might be a distraction. What this means for twentieth-century Christians is that we cannot hope to fulfill the biblical demand for justice and love by imitating the social institutions of twenty centuries ago, but are called instead to examine our own institutions and mores in the light of the City of God. Marriage is Christian not when it conforms to law, from which we have been set free, but when it becomes *sacrament.*

We believe that in the freely chosen union of man and woman, they find mutual joy, comfort in sorrow and pain, and a setting for the raising of children. More than that, however, the sacramental nature of marriage means that this union is holy: We can see something of God in it. As we come to understand more fully God's self-giving love, a love which abandons power in favor of vulnerability, Christian marriages will conform themselves to that image of God. Dominance has no place in a Christian marriage. It is replaced by service to one another. Some scholars call the product of such a marriage based on mutual care and openness to sharing one another's pain the "symmetrical family." In such a marriage, husband and wife undertake to support one another and to share in the joy and pain of nurturing not only one another but their children.

The mutuality and sacrificial service which embody the love of God in a Christian marriage define the setting in which human dignity and justice come to their fulfillment and contradict the ideology of the Christian Right which would find God only in domination and power.

Desirable as that goal might be, however, some do not succeed in making it real for themselves. Ideological Christians on the Right have no place for them, since they are viewed as deviants from the norms imposed by God. William Barnwell, a divorced priest, observes that both homosexuals and divorced people find themselves beyond the norms not only of society but of the New Testament. He suggests, however, that the scripture indicates that like Adam and Eve when they were banished from the Garden, they will find that God will meet them where they are and assure them of dignity and protection: "God promises to help us make the best of our situation."[49]

Such theological affirmations can help the church as it finds itself on the threshold of exploring the implications of justice and dignity for those who, perhaps through no fault of their own, find that they do not conform to the ideal of permanent marriage—more than half the population of the United States by 1980. What principles can help us move beyond the ideology of the New Right to a genuinely biblical ethic based on love and justice?

Christians are right to affirm the permanence of freely chosen marriages built on mutual commitment and love which respects both wife and husband. Only such a marriage can be said to embody and reflect fully the justice of God. Such households are indeed "havens of blessing and peace," a prelude to the City of God. But is the cause of justice served by insisting that all marriages are "forever," if to do so perpetuates the violence and abuse which afflict so many households? Was Jesus' own attitude towards divorce shaped by his concern to defend the rights of women when society had no place for single people, and might there be circumstances in our time when a similar concern might argue *for,* not *against,* divorce? Are there occasions when God's demand for justice might be better served by divorce? Is marriage excluded from the promise of forgiveness and the chance to begin over again? What exactly does it mean for a husband and wife to be "one in Christ Jesus"?

Just as the Christian Right's image of marriage fails to do justice to a critical reading of history and scripture, its attitude towards homosexuality is neither biblical nor based on a uniform reading of Christian tradition.

Almost all Old Testament scholars now agree that the so-called sin of Sodom so important to fundamentalists was not homosexuality at all, but inhospitality. Leviticus's prohibition rests on the fact that homosexual acts were popularly identified with pagan worship. Jesus never once mentions the subject. Although there are three references in Paul's epistles which might refer to homosexual behavior, the meaning of the Greek words in two of them is uncertain; the Revised Standard Version chooses words like *impurity* which seem not to have any reference to homosexuality at all. The one case where Paul does specifically condemn homosexual activity (Romans 1:26–27) has to do with *heterosexuals* who seek out relations with members of their own sex. The Bible seems never to address or consider homosexuality as a condition or orientation, focusing entirely on the acts themselves.

A critical look at Christian history indicates an ambiguous and complex attitude towards homosexuality through the centuries. John Boswell's recent study, *Christianity, Social Tolerance and Homosexuality* finds no evidence that the early Christians opposed homosexual behavior. Contrary to the generally accepted belief that homosexuality prevailed during the decline of the Roman Empire and contributed to its collapse, the evidence indicates that it flourished during the classical period and that as the Empire waned, both church and state moved towards an antihomosexual position, rigorously legislating matters of personal morality as Europe's urban culture declined and the church preached an increasingly ascetic form of Christianity. When city life revived in the eleventh century, homosexuality again appeared in Europe; homosexuals "were prominent, influential and respected at many levels of society in most of Europe, and left a permanent mark on the cultural monuments of the age, both religious and secular."[50] Between 1150 and 1350, however, attitudes again changed. In 1100, Boswell observes, even figures close to the pope could not prevent the election of a homosexual bishop; by 1300, "a single homosexual act was enough to prevent absolutely ordination to any clerical rank, to render one liable to persecution by ecclesiastical courts, or—in many places—to merit the death penalty."[51]

Boswell is uncertain why the antihomosexual passion unleashed in Europe during the Middle Ages took such a form, but notes that it occurred at a period when all minorities—Jews, other non-Christians, heretics, and those suspected of witchcraft—came under steady and virulent persecution. The sentiment in medieval Europe was less a matter of theology or reason than of prejudice and passion.

The same might be said of the Moral Majority's position. Saint Paul seems to consider homosexual behavior to be on an ethical par with anger, envy, and carousing (see Galatians 5:19ff.); Falwell places it in a category and a level of abomination all its own, and claims that it is a freely chosen state which begins with seduction and ends with addiction. "Homosexuals," he asserts, "cannot reproduce themselves, so they must recruit."[52] Such statements contradict almost every serious study of homosexuality, which indicate that sexual orientation is not a matter of conscious choice, that it is established extremely early in life, that it can be changed only rarely, that its causes are unknown and probably multiple, that the overwhelming majority of child molesters are heterosexual, and that as many as half of all homosexuals are married, many of them also parents. The Moral Majority's image of homosexuality and its ideological stance help prevent Christians from grappling with the real issue, which is how the biblical promises of justice and love apply to people whose sexuality is oriented towards the same sex.

The Christian Right would have us believe that the marriage bond is summed up in power. Christians who search out the Bible's prophetic message find values far more important in the call for justice and the demand for love and dignity for all God's people. A God who surrendered power for love calls us to do the same. Christians are called to hold up those enduring values within every human relationship, confident that in fulfilling God's demands, we will move beyond ideology to faith.

## ⚬ 6 ⚬

# The Church of the Air Waves

"The most important reason The Christian Broadcasting Network exists is to spread the gospel of Jesus Christ to all the world."
—Pat Robertson[1]

"The 'electronic church' is a heretical movement and a danger to Biblical Christianity because it denies the essentiality of the organized church."
—Mark R. Sills[2]

The church plays a pivotal function in the Moral Majority's world view; but not surprisingly, Christians on the Right give a somewhat specialized meaning to their use of the word *church*. It seems to have almost nothing to do with the many denominational traditions to which most American Christians give allegiance; nor, for that matter, is it primarily concerned with the local gathering of Christians in a congregation. Rather, the church seems not to be an institution at all. It is instead a loosely organized movement, led by a number of independent, self-appointed preachers, of those who profess a fundamentalist version of Christian faith which has been with Americans since the Great Awakening. With few exceptions, these clergy have only the most tenuous ties with groups beyond their own enterprise, and their ministry is aimed not at a specific community but at an audience determined by their media outlets and with a national or even international potential. Many of them challenge their viewers with the vision of a movement global in scope: Pat Robertson reminds his followers that "for the first time in the history of the world we now have the technology through satellite communications to, indeed, preach the gospel in all the world."[3]

Not all the television preachers fit the same mold or share the viewpoint of the Moral Majority. Some, like Robertson and Falwell, are closely identified with the social and political agenda of the New Right; others, like Robert Schuller, associate freely with political leaders whom the Right views with horror and are more closely identified with the nonpolitical evangelism which antedated the revival of populist Christian politics. Schuller is an immaculately coiffed, articulate, cherubic figure whose "Crystal Cathedral" verges on opulence and who calls celebrities by their first name. Jimmy Swaggart speaks in the passionate tones and uncertain grammar of an old-fashioned tent preacher. Both Schuller and Falwell set their programs in the context of a congregation. (Falwell's Thomas Road Baptist Church in Lynchburg, Virginia, claims eighteen thousand members in a city of just over seventy thousand. Schuller's Crystal Cathedral is noted not only for its religion but is also a remarkable example of contemporary California architecture.) Swaggart specializes in the traditional mass meetings which have played such an important role in popular religion of the South and West. Robertson's "700 Club" and Jim Bakker's "PTL ('Praise the Lord') Club" follow the familiar format of the talk-and-variety show. What all have in common is a personable, "popular" style, and a primary commitment to a television audience. Whatever setting they choose, they use the medium in such a way that the viewer has the illusion of being addressed *personally* and *individually*. This sense of rapport between preacher and viewer is amplified by numerous techniques. Viewers are encouraged to speak to a program staff member by long-distance telephone, or to correspond with the preacher. Viewers can obtain special envelopes for submitting private requests for prayer. Thanks to computer mailing, letters from their headquarters often address the recipient by first name and are almost invariably signed in the same way. Nicknames are the norm: Pat Robertson, Jim Bakker, Jimmy Swaggart. The setting of a mass audience as background may give viewers the vicarious sense of being present, an illusion fostered by the preacher, whose attention shifts constantly between the camera and the "live" audience. Of course individuals also have the opportunity to be personally involved in the ministry through financial support—the more generous, the deeper the feeling of participation. Several of the preachers promote "membership" in their programs. Pat Robertson's "700 Club" members pledge at least fifteen dollars monthly, in return for which they receive a magazine, a monthly newsletter interpreting current events, a cassette recording, membership card and "certificate suitable for framing," "and a gold-tone '700 Club' collar/lapel pin." [4] One viewer who testifies to watching Jerry Falwell's broadcast three times a week adds, "I am sure he doesn't want me to do otherwise." [5] Such viewers are the true "congregation" for these preachers, and the backbone of what has been called the "electronic church." Local congregations might well support the program of the television preachers, but they are secondary to the company of faithful individual viewers on whom they depend. The constant refrain of Robert Schuller's written and spoken message is "God loves you—and so do I." It seems as if the anonymity of the television camera were transformed in the face of such sincerity.

For more than two centuries, mass-audience preachers have been a fixture of populist Christianity. They carried the Great Awakening from town to town, and were the central figures of the frontier camp meetings. They provided "revivals" to boost the flagging spirits of thousands or even millions of people in churches across America. With the advent of the twentieth-century mass media, their potential audience grew to vast proportions; but it is only in recent years that their ministry has shifted from the role of *augmenting* to that of *replacing* the local church. Of course, none of the television preachers would ever advise their viewers against congregational worship, and many encourage it. Yet studies indicate that mass evangelism has almost no effect in motivating people to participate in corporate forms of church life. A study released in 1978 by the Institute for American Church Growth revealed that of the hundreds of thousands of "decisions for Christ" registered by the Campus Crusade for Christ, only 3 *percent* of the converts were ever incorporated into a congregation.[6] Among the more than sixty million Americans who are unchurched, fully 64 percent believe that Jesus is God or the Son of God, and 76 percent affirm that they pray.[7] These nominal but unattached Christians provide an enormous potential for a viewing audience who will never come near a church but who consider their faith fulfilled through their support of, and loyalty to, the television preacher(s) of their choice.

The income generated by the television preachers is worth noting. The annual receipts from Falwell's "Old-Fashioned Gospel Hour" total $60 million, only slightly higher than the Christian Broadcasting Network's $58 million. The "PTL Club" generates $25 million per year, the "700 Club" $30 million, and Robert Schuller's "Hour of Power" $11 million. Most of the $16 million to build the Crystal Cathedral came not from those who attend it but from Schuller's television audience.[8]

This formidable ability to raise money in small amounts from numerous sources represents one way in which the electronic church has benefited from the skills developed by figures like Richard Viguerie. Its success depends on electronic technology and the effective utilization of both mass mailing and television itself.

The most effective of the television preachers have been trained or were gifted with an unusual natural ability to use the media as a means of communicating a sense of confidence and vigor as well as the illusion of personal concern for a faceless audience. Their message, implied or articulated, is that by following their advice viewers will find themselves among those for whom "faith really paid off."[9]

Worship in the electronic church is not corporate but private, not participatory but designed for spectators who observe from their own homes.

> Thank you, Dr. Schuller. Every Sunday morning my wife and I sit by the television with a cup of coffee and listen to your beautiful lecture. Now, when I'm away from home, which happens most of the time, I will listen in my hotel room and she will listen at home.[10]

The messages which are the focal point of electronic worship are both *evangelistic,* aimed at the conversion which traditionally begins the evangelical Christian's life of faith, and also *testimonial,* offering the witness of committed Christians to illuminate the ways in which faith shapes everyday life. Preaching is punctuated by appeals for financial support, many of which offer gifts or reading matter in return, and by occasional music. The music may take the form of old-fashioned hymns well known by the audience; the melody and setting are often nearly indistinguishable from contemporary popular music, but the words tend to be simple, easily remembered affirmations of faith.

Electronic preaching follows one or more predictable styles, some familiar to populist Christianity, others of them innovative. Like revivalist preachers of other times, the television evangelists are extremely fond of retelling the stories of conversion.

One of Schuller's witnesses recounts: "I imagine that during my life I probably did 300 LSD trips. I consider myself a very fortunate man just to be standing here. . . . But drugs took the bottom out of my life. I wound up penniless and broke." Conversion turned his life around, however, and very soon he and his wife decided to heed Schuller's advice and tithe. "That very week God delivered to our family a complete house of furniture! . . . Two weeks later the Lord gave us a beautiful two-bedroom house for the same amount of rental money, complete with a swimming pool in the front yard. God has a marvellous accounting system!"[11]

The television preachers are evangelists of a gospel that "works." They often imply that loyalty to God and faithful contributions to those who are doing the Lord's work will "pay off" in numerous ways. Many of them make a habit of parading a series of "successful" people who are willing to identify themselves as "born-again Christians" and who seem to believe that, far from being a liability, Christianity can be an enormous resource in getting ahead. As one businessman commented to Robert Schuller: "From a purely self-interest point of view, ethics pay off. The ethical responsibility of a company and the people within it, represent the basis upon which any successful business is founded. . . . The successful business leaders I know are sensitive people. They build their businesses by recognizing the sensitivity of the egos of other people, and the self-esteem needs of those people."[12]

This functional theology is at the heart of the appeal of the star television preachers. The desire for security, for confidence and a sense of belonging, for a "handle" on life—in a word, for *power*—can be identified clearly by a glance at the publications and tapes offered for sale by Schuller's organization: They offer advice on "power to make your dreams come true," "your key to lasting happiness," "the success system that really works," "daily power thoughts."[13] Perhaps the ultimate reward is held out by Pat Robertson to his viewers. Reminding them that the end will come only when the gospel has been preached to the whole world, he hints that contributing to his program will actually hasten the day of Christ's return.[14]

The promise of unspecified rewards in return for financial support and personal loyalty carries no penalties. Whatever happens or fails to happen, the viewers have only themselves to blame; if they had given more, prayed harder, believed more fervently, things would have been different. Faith turns inward, not outward; personal change and adjustment take precedence over changing the world we live in, even when it is responsible for our pain. The mission is to America and the world, but the life of faith is nurtured in countless individual souls who never meet. The preachers of the airwaves have called a new kind of church into being: a church whose members never see or touch each other.

That invisible body of alienated and lonely people, cut off from a sense of helping shape their lives and their world, has always been the breeding ground of discontent from which American populism grows. That movement in turn has celebrated the fundamentalist values and beliefs of its supporters. It is no wonder that when the New Right revives those old populist attitudes, some segments of the electronic church should be attracted to the content of their program. Nor is it surprising that the New Right should seek support from the television preachers. After all, the populist Right and the electronic church address the same following; they speak the same language and preach the same values; they thrive on the same kinds of discontent.

### Television and the Body of Christ

For two thousand years, Christians have understood faith in the context of membership in the Body of Christ. The sacrament of baptism grafts us into the Body and makes us living members of the corporate household of faith. We are nurtured through its sacraments, worship in its company, bear one another's burdens, and as we mature in faith, we grow more deeply into communion not only with Christ but with one another. It is of the very essence of membership in the church that we know and participate in its corporate life. Paul's epistles abound in references to our membership in the body: It is the foretaste of life in the City of God. The Christian community is called to be the mirror and vision of what is to come, the destiny of humankind. We are the people who show forth the resurrection of Christ in our own common life. We are fed with that risen life whenever we eat bread and drink wine together in the Eucharist. We experience forgiveness and healing in the community. Our faith comes to fruition in the life we share with the Body of Christ. Each of us has our own special gifts which make us matter to its life. Without concrete love for our brothers and sisters nurtured and strengthened in the church, our love for God is an illusion. *We find our relationship with God in and through our relationships with others.* Our life in the church is not peripheral to our Christian faith, it is essential. From the New Testament's perspective, we meet Christ in the community which is his Body. Faith is a private affair, but it comes to fruition only in community. Conversion to Christ is fulfilled when we find him in one another.

What the preachers of the electronic church proclaim is a distorted Christianity which suggests that we no longer need the church-in-the-flesh. Mark Sills comments that such preaching implies that "the Body of Christ does not need to be incarnate in a particular community through an organized congregation. . . . Instead it substitutes a massive *appearance* of community scattered all across the land through the use of modern technology." Like the ancient heresy of Docetism, which claimed that Jesus only *appeared* to be a real man, the electronic church is "a seeming church having only spirit but no body. It is a 'communion of saints' without having the sacrament of true communion. It is a 'fellowship of believers' without having any concrete interaction, a phantom fellowship of the mind alone. It is a 'body of Christ' without a corpus, a body consisting only of a head but having no arms, no legs, no heart!"[15]

Just as God's presence in the world required a body of flesh and blood, the church has no meaning or identity unless it has a body. The illusory church of the media can offer neither sacramental communion nor the communion of shared life. For all its opportunities for financial support, it does not offer commitment to real human beings, which is the stuff of true faith. William Fore, communications secretary for the National Council of Churches, suggests that it is "substituting an anonymous (and therefore undemanding) commitment for the kind of person-to-person involvement and group commitment that is the essence of the local church."[16] That local congregation is, after all, "still the place where people are able to meet and work out their salvation together. It is still the place where the history of the saints can be appropriated, where the biblical symbols, visions and images manage to come through, where people together can still take a stand."[17]

The disembodied television church is powerless to witness to its society. In spite of the Christian Right's attacks on aspects of American culture which displease them, their campaigns have the same impersonality as their worship. Their instruments are the postcard and the phone call; they lack the possibility of corporate grappling with the injustice and violence which haunt us all. If they are familiar with the loneliness of millions of Americans, they lack the means to address it except to smile on camera. They know the needs of their audience: "to be recognized, to be needed, to live in a world that can be understood, to be of worth, to be secure."[18] But because there is no community, those needs cannot be addressed in any genuine way.

Because it is meant to mirror the City of God, the church has a calling to put into practice the justice and freedom which are God's intention for us. There are two dimensions to this vocation. The first is to create within its own community a society of believers who enjoy the dignity to which God entitles them, who are noticed and heard and respected and loved, and who are agents of God's love for one another. Paul was quite clear about this mission. We are to model our life within the Christian community in such a way that it provides a preview of what the City of God will be like. The church is to be a household not of power but of love, not of lost and lonely people but of responsible and free men and women. The inequalities and injustices of this world have no place in the Body of Christ.

The other side of our vocation is to be agents of God's justice and compassion in the world. The church is to address the world as it is in the name of its vision of what it might become. It is therefore called to be *prophetic,* challenging the powers that be to live up to the possibilities which God has given us in our very humanness. In a world where oppression and hopelessness abound, the church which is faithful to its Good News speaks a powerful word of hope and a call to freedom. A church which lives out such a vocation meets *real* human need, because it lives in the real world. The electronic church is invisible and other-worldly.

The reason is that there are no *people* in the electronic church, only performers and spectators, images and the nameless. The wholeness of the Body of Christ, and its mission beyond itself, depend upon the presence of flesh-and-blood humanity: old and young, women and men, laypeople and clergy, each with talents and functions to perform within the Body. That corporate wholeness can be distorted easily enough even in a church as earthy as ours. Clergy sometimes assume to themselves the prerogatives of power and relegate everyone else to second-class citizenship in the City of God. For most of its life, the church's men have dominated its women, even when, for all practical purposes, it was the women who kept the institution going. Sometimes we overlook the children, or the elderly, or the unattached. But the presence of the whole spectrum of humankind in the Body tends to keep it from being permanently deformed. When popes and prelates become too corrupt, a Francis appears to shame them. When they become timid and comfortable, a Catherine or a Teresa challenges them to live up to their calling. When we become too stuffy, God graces us with a John Wesley, or charms us with a performance of *Godspell.* If we forget our mission, a Martin Luther King revives the dream. If women are judged to be somehow unworthy as priests in the church of God, sooner or later there will be those who know better and are not afraid to fulfill their calling. This vision of the church *"semper reformanda,"* "always being reformed," as Martin Luther put it, depends upon the constant interaction of faithful men and women in a real-life Body. Without that contact, conversation, and even controversy, the church is distorted almost beyond recognition.

Just such a distorted communion now exists among the believers who are bound together only by their prejudices and their televisions. The church has been reduced among them to a collection of isolated consumers, seeking security and confidence in a difficult, lonely, and painful age. "How do you find that confident faith?" asks Robert Schuller. "By following the kind of leader who can give it to you."[19] Paul had a very different answer. "For freedom," he wrote, "Christ has set us free; stand fast, therefore, and do not submit again to a yoke of slavery."[20]

The electronic church puts an untold amount of power into the hands of its preachers. Indeed, for all practical purposes, they live and work without any accountability except to those viewers who provide or withhold the funds they need. They are innocent of any framework of shared responsibility, and exercise their ministry as arbiters of morality at a level which medieval popes would envy. Their word determines ethical principles, acceptable modes of social behavior, taste, and style; when they also identify with the New Right, they proclaim a political party line as strict as any commissar's. At their nod torrents of mail flood Congress and the White House, and a hint of displeasure can sever sponsorship of a national television program lest their anger bear fruit in the marketplace. The conservative theologian and sociologist Peter Berger observes that they share a "religious and political certitude which, despite all ideological differences, is uncomfortably reminiscent of the fanaticism unleashed by Muslim fundamentalists."[21] "If one says of a particular political position," he notes, "that it and no other is the will of God, one is implicitly excommunicating those who disagree."[22]

What makes their certainties more dangerous is that in the church as they define and experience it, there is no one to challenge them. The elementary demands of justice and compassion to which we are called as citizens of God's City are directed to the church as to the world. No image of the church which invests all spiritual power in the hands of so few is true to the Body of Christ as Paul described it.

Nor is preaching which promises power and success acquainted with the cross. The show-business church's repeated insistence that "prayer works," that faithfulness and obedience will be rewarded by financial or personal success and happiness, is a monumental distortion of the New Testament. Jesus promises no success, only tribulation. Any ultimate improvement in our situation must await the arrival of God's City; here we have only glimpses of that future. Indeed, Jesus often warned his friends that following him might do nothing for them except to get them in trouble. We are promised persecution, arrest, physical discomfort, hatred, and violence; the specter of death itself is hinted as a possibility. Furthermore, respectability and the company of the powerful is described as a temptation: "Woe to you when all speak well of you; so their parents did to the false prophets."[23]

The later New Testament figures found that Jesus' predictions were absolutely accurate. He had, as he warned, brought not peace but a sword. The long catalogues of mistreatment Paul shared with his readers were not the exception but the rule. It is a sign of their selective and ideological reading of the scriptures that the television preachers can offer us more than Jesus ever promised.

Christ's gift is something altogether different: "For freedom Christ has set us free." That terrifying gift becomes bearable only in a church in which we share our joy and pain with one another. Only a church which brings us together is worthy of the name.

# 7

# Whose Theology?

"The Moral Majority is neither."
—*A button slogan*

Different styles of theology lead to very different consequences. *Ideology* is a way of describing what is real which claims to be a revelation of "the way things are." We can see this kind of theology at work on a simple level in the ancient legends and folktales which peoples pass down to tell their children how things came to be. Theology of this kind often imagines a "master plan" for all things, laid down at the dawn of creation and imposing order and purpose on what would otherwise be a universe of chaos. Such reflection takes for granted that the way to survive in the world won't change very much. Ideology is a set of beliefs and actions which tell us what we may expect from the world and how to conform to it. Such theology lends itself to a religion of rules, in which we find a way to get by without bringing down destruction on ourselves; at best, we can even "work" the rules to our own advantage.

An alternative, *critical* method of theology considers that truth and its consequences can never be separated. It takes seriously the everyday world as we know it, but measures it against what it might be, offering something new and better. When theology is based on such hints of a future which is different from the present, it enables us to see how reality might be something else than it appears. Such theology is critical, not in the sense that it sees only the negative, but in the primary sense of the word, which means that it can make judgments and choices about what is and what might be. It is *prophetic* because it is shaped by the future rather than by what has always been.

Christians on the Right claim to base their program on a biblical theology; but in fact, they use the Bible ideologically, to buttress a view of reality which is unchanging and absolute. The scriptures, on the other hand, show us a God interested not in abstract revelation but in how people live. In particular, God cares about *love*—love in the sense of caring about the well-being of another. Justice is not something else again; it is love made flesh. Justice is the condition in which people have what they need, and it is the state the Bible assumes we are all to experience.

Theology explains reality in terms of what really matters. It is always critical: It is true if, and only if, it brings to pass those values for which Christ died. The religion it fosters is more concerned with ends than with rules: "Pure religion and undefiled before God and the Father is this: to visit orphans and widows in their affliction, and to keep oneself unstained from the world."[1]

Ideology claims to be an unbiased view of reality, while critical theology does not hesitate to reveal that it is biased in favor of those who most need love and justice. The truth is, there is no such thing as "value-free" theology. All theology is in someone's favor. The only question is *whom* it benefits.

While claiming to be objective, the former style in fact supports those with the most power. The "divine right of kings" is an excellent example of such a theological principle. By identifying monarchy with "the way things are" and therefore God's will, the support of religion was guaranteed to whoever was on the throne. Questions of justice and tyranny were irrelevant. Only the second, critical, style of theology has the potential for serving true justice, because it is willing to examine not only what theology *says* but how it *works*.

Both Jesus and the prophets before him knew well that it is possible to practice religion without seeking justice. Amos was familiar with people who tried to practice their religion with the minimum distraction from what really interested them, which was making money. Jesus knew that some of his neighbors dedicated their property to God—which cost them nothing—as a way to avoid the obligation of caring for their parents. Their religion was *formally* correct—they "kept the rules"—but their intention was not to secure justice or practice compassion, but to circumvent both. Few people felt Jesus' wrath more fully. Clearly, he considered that it was impossible to evaluate religion without asking what, and for whom, it was for. It is not meant for our own personal gain but for the cause of love and justice. The *only* judgment which interested Jesus was that which notes our behavior towards the hungry, the thirsty, the poor, the sick, and the oppressed.[2]

Our evaluation of the Christian Right and its theology would be incomplete without questioning both the way it works and for whom it works. We must ask, therefore: Whom does the Moral Majority address? Whom does it serve? And because all theology has a bias, we must also note whom it is against, and whom it might harm. We need to discover whether its biases correspond to those of Jesus and the Bible. Finally, we must ask ourselves, Does this theology work? Does it succeed in making sense of the world and in meeting the needs of its adherents, from their own perspective and from that of Jesus himself?

### The Moral Majority and Its Audience

Like the populists of every age, the Moral Majority speaks to people who consider themselves to be alienated from those who control America and excluded from the culture which belongs to the class in power. Because those who wield economic, political, and cultural power tend to be urban, concentrated on the coasts and especially in the Northeast, there is a geographical component to the New Right's appeal. It is directed primarily towards people who live outside the cities, and it finds most of its audience in the South and West. The Moral Majority is aware that it has potential supporters even in metropolis; it views their situation much like that of the Chosen People in captivity. Falwell and his associates make periodic forays into cities like New York, but they do so with the air of saints treading gingerly and distastefully through Babylon. It is obvious to all, supporters and opponents alike, that the city is alien territory.

American populism has always distrusted intellectuals. The Protestant fundamentalism which forms its religious base is actually defined in part by its opposition to rationalism and secular learning. Populists have always known that knowledge is power, and have been acutely aware that the academic community tends to support and ally itself with the "power elite." In recent years, not only knowledge but, more specifically, *learning* is power. Both the technology on which modern life depends and the bureaucracy which keeps our institutions functioning call for specific kinds of academic preparation. We even speak now of a "knowledge industry." The Moral Majority addresses those who, through no fault of their own, remain isolated from the kinds of learning associated with access to power. There is no disguising the glee which Falwell and his congregation share when he ridicules the scientists whom they consider their enemy. Yet their scorn cannot entirely hide their realization that, in important ways, they are not themselves "in the know" and that they suffer from it.

Because they are themselves excluded from power, the Christian Right's audience tends to a negative collective and individual self-image. Much of their posturing reveals how deeply they identify themselves as victims. Their belligerence and even rage mask a sense of inferiority which comes from being aware of an alienation that is not supposed to exist at all. Their ideology of America is based on equality of opportunity and the myth of the classless society; the experience of the people to whom the Moral Majority speaks is otherwise. They *know* that some rule and others are ruled, and they cannot help but sense the odds that prevent them from gaining real power over their own lives. Yet the only hope that saves them from despair is the belief, irrational in that it is unsupported by evidence, that the Horatio Alger myth of virtue and hard work rewarded can still come true for them.

Their determination to preserve that myth lies behind the Moral Majority's "conservative" intentions. It is not that the old ways have worked for them, and they have certainly not arrived at their beliefs by logical or objective analysis. It is just that no other alternative seems real or possible. Their uncritical celebration of America and their angry patriotism could be seen as the sign of a desperate need for faith in the only hope they have, and a plea for security in a world which seems to offer very little in the way of certainty. How fragile that faith is can be observed if we will only note the millenarianism which pervades right-wing Christianity.

Perhaps Christians in the mainstream have not been sufficiently sensitive to the meaning of such a faith. Right-wing Christians are fervent about the expected return of Christ because they genuinely believe that they live in "the worst of times," times so bad that only Christ's return could explain them or improve them. Apocalyptic faith is actually a function of despair.

Populism customarily attracts people who play by the rules and yet do not prosper, or if they do, are nevertheless excluded from real power. Because they cannot dare to question the rules themselves, they are always on the lookout for someone to blame for their failure. They work hard but remain on the lower rungs of the economic and social ladder. The Moral Majority attracts people from the working class and the lower middle class rather than those who are the poorest at the bottom.

Those poor, migrants and alien workers, racial minorities in the urban ghettos and the rural poor of all races, are not attracted to the Moral Majority even though they share its fundamentalism. They decline to play by the rules which so fascinate the Christian Right, because they *know* they don't work for them. Racism, the welfare system, and the forgetfulness of our economics and politics guarantee that the ordinary mythologies of success and upward mobility do not apply to them. They live apart from the social consensus, in one of the many subcultures of poverty (or, at worst, apart from society's values altogether in the private prison of the psychopath). Different values, based not on power but on survival, dominate the life of the poorest Americans.

But the populists pledge allegiance to the middle class to which they aspire and to which they look for security, even as they rage at their exclusion. If the Moral Majority hates those in power for ignoring them, it hates those poorer than they even more, because it is the poor who tell them, in effect, that they are wasting their time, that the "traditional" America they yearn for is what excluded them in the first place, and that the rules insure that they will continue to be powerless.

The prosperity of the period between World War II and the mid-1970s raised living standards and expectations for many Americans. At the same time, the changing shape of our economy meant that more people were employed in better-paying white-collar jobs in the bureaucracy necessary to maintain our institutions and our commerce. Yet their entrance into what appeared to be the middle class did not give them a sense of power or "belonging." Even with advanced training and academic degrees, the members of this new social group are not entrepreneurs or managers but employees. They form a white-collar working class even if they earn fifty thousand dollars a year.

This disgruntled group has been disappointed by affluence. They are shocked to find that it is possible to live in split-level suburbs, own two expensive cars, and still feel victimized by power beyond their control. They may work for a mammoth corporation whose mindless processes treat them as if they were only bits of machinery. They are painfully aware that their jobs are neither productive nor satisfying. Their position is tenuous, depending not on personal bonds or the claims of fairness but on their continued profitability for their employer.

This better-educated, more well-heeled population has become part of the potential audience for the New Right because they still lack what they want. The institutions on which they counted seem to be fragmented and out of control. Their high incomes have brought neither security, nor power, nor happiness, nor peace. Their families are dissolving; their children are beyond their understanding and may be drinking heavily or wallowing in adolescent promiscuity and drugs. Their fear that unforeseen events may destroy their precarious wealth and position on the ladder makes them cheer a bellicose America. They long for the "good old days" of their imagination because it seems as if they offered stability and security. They cannot believe that what looked so certain and attractive from a distance could always have been as fragile and unsatisfying as it seems up close. And they dare not ask themselves if perhaps the middle-class goal of their dreams could itself have been the product of fantasy.

The alienation and fear which are the raw material of populist politics and religion live on among that movement's traditional audience, but they are now joined by this new constituency for the Moral Majority's attentions. They are people who look as if they "belong" but who are in fact lonely and afraid, who want and need power to shape their own lives—power over their own fate.

## Bias on the Right

The audience to which the Christian Right addresses itself is certain that the world is a difficult and painful place. The question which must be asked is whether its image of that world corresponds to reality, and if what the Moral Majority has to offer can in fact produce what they need. They proclaim a "traditional" America, a "conservative" religion, an "old-fashioned" family. But whom in fact does their faith serve?

The frontier attitude which considers that there is always room to move "up and out," and which depends upon infinite capacities for growth as both possible and desirable, has not yet come to terms with the reality of an America limited by resources, by world events, and by other poles of power which shape the destiny of our planet. Indeed, the New Right denies that there are any boundaries at all. We might recall William Simon's plaintive message quoted in Chapter Four that prosperity is waiting to be "unleashed." But wishing doesn't make it so. An uncontrolled *laissez-faire* economy of the kind Simon and the New Right preach was based upon small, independent, privately owned family enterprises in which all competed on more or less equal terms. To call for such an economic system in an age like ours insures the flourishing not of individual initiative but its destruction by mighty industrial giants which transcend nationality and bypass the checks and balances which give economics a human face. Such an ideology, if put fully into practice, would remove all restraints from those who already have the lion's share of power. Their power would then be absolute. The last vestige of hope for the survival of human values over against pure profit would be gone.

The anxiety of the Right and its refuge in an image of America as sheer power works most to the benefit of those whose livelihood depends upon such a warlike posture. The image of "fortress America" feeds industries which are among the most profitable and successful. The "military-industrial complex," to use Eisenhower's familiar phrase, is not imaginary. A significant portion of our business and manufacturing community is in fact dedicated to the "security" enterprise. Workers in those industries very often need highly specialized knowledge, and command incomes far greater than most working people will ever see. Defense-related industry and the military establishment are perhaps the chief beneficiaries of an uncritical appeal for an invincible state which is never safe enough. That fact in itself ought to make us wary of the objectivity of calls for constantly improved technologies of death. Christians may lack the technical knowledge necessary to evaluate the relative value of military systems and needs. But we can at least raise the question of whom such a policy benefits, and call it by its proper name. We can lose sight of the real purpose of weaponry and armed forces when we speak of "defense." We are really talking about the ability to kill.

Apart from the technological and esthetic desirability of living under an economy dominated by its dedication to the potential for violence and destruction, even conservative economists admit that military spending is one of the chief causes of inflation in the United States. A conspiracy of silence hinders the full discussion of the implications of that fact, but the truth is, such spending diverts human and natural resources from productive labor. Money and workers who could be dedicated to goods and services which in turn generate more wealth and employment are employed instead in the stockpiling of arms which are meant never to be used and which have only destructive functions. It takes neither special wisdom nor imagination to understand why such unexamined policy causes inflation.

We should also note that inflation is not an enemy which deals equally with everyone. It is dangerous for the poor, whose income rises less rapidly than prices, and to working people, whose savings decline during inflation. It is devastating to the elderly, whose income is often fixed permanently at the time of retirement. It is least dangerous, and often even advantageous, to the rich and to those whose personal finances are complex enough to put the declining value of the dollar to work for them.

Nor should we overlook the fact that uncontrolled military spending and unbridled corporate growth alike generate a small army of "experts" whose arcane knowledge places them in a position not unlike that of the alchemists of the Middle Ages.

They were rumored to have sacred knowledge that would be of great use to anyone in search of power and riches, and possessed wisdom unfathomable by "ordinary" folk. Although the New Right knows well that the purveyors of such knowledge exclude them, it is bound to an ideology that guarantees their faithful allegiance to a point of view that exalts such "experts."

That kind of irony pervades the Christian Right, in that it supports an ideology which claims to speak for victimized people, but in fact serves no one except those already in power— and the preachers and advocates who have learned to make money from the movement itself. Successful proclamation of the gospel according to the Moral Majority may do very little to meet the needs of its audience. But those who do it persuasively enough may find themselves caught up in a world of private jets, pillared mansions, and manicured gardens, clutching their King James Bible in their hand, still speaking to and for the real majority of Americans for whom such a world exists only in fantasy.

The Moral Majority cannot give its followers what they want or need. It tells women that their place is in the home, yet supports economics which, by feeding inflation, makes a mockery of the possibility of staying at home for women who care about the economic survival of their family. It preaches the myth of success, thereby guaranteeing that people will fail to understand the need for the power that really matters, which is power to shape their own lives. It acclaims the family, yet absolutizes an image of the relationship between the sexes which makes love and intimacy nearly impossible, furthering the collapse of the one institution most designed to affirm mutual dignity and support. By rejecting the possibility of rapprochement between Christianity and secular learning, it confines its version of Christian faith to a cultural ghetto, and forces children to vacillate wildly between two kinds of learning, one empirical, the other irrational.

And what of those "others," the "least" on whose behalf Jesus spoke? What of the aged, bereft of economic hope in their old age, distanced by miles and culture from the children who ignore them, on whom inflation takes the worst toll, and for whom illness is an unaffordable nightmare? If "fortress America" forgets them in order to build bigger bombs, to whom shall they turn?

The poor are least equipped to compete for declining jobs; their incomes rise less rapidly than prices in periods of inflation. At what point do they despair? When they cannot pay the rent? When they can no longer feed their children? When it becomes economically preferable to abandon work for welfare? Their parents could always find menial work at the bottom of the ladder, but that rung has grown smaller and more crowded. Washing machines, dishwashers, and power mowers have made their skills obsolete. Even our elevators are usually self-service. When there are no jobs for the poor, what are they to do? What does the Moral Majority have to offer them?

What about the young? We enjoy calling them the "future of America." With the cost of a college education approaching forty or fifty thousand dollars, what will become of them? As *laissez-faire* turns a blind eye to their problems, when they no longer see any hope of achieving the experience and training they must have, what will the Christian Right say to them?

What about the fate of the minorities who still suffer the legacy of slavery and discrimination? Having struggled at great cost towards the dignity and freedom most of us inherited, having fought for the laws which made possible their entrance into the mainstream, they note anxiously that the New Right now demands an end to "favoritism." Does this mean that racism and prejudice are to be "decontrolled"? No wonder that William Jones, president of the National Black Pastors' Conference, charged Falwell with preaching a "theology of tribalism" which equates "piety with patriotism." He reminded Falwell that blacks did not "recall your presence when we had to contend so mightily for racial justice in America. . . . We did not hear your voice when vile and vicious racists challenged our right of access to the basics of life."[3]

Jones is right. The ideology of power on which the Moral Majority rests is a theory for the social survival of the fittest. It guarantees that those who are most vulnerable will be forgotten. Jesus knew of such ideologies, but he assumed that when others forgot, his followers would be the people who remember. When factions fan social strife and accept division as right and natural, the biblical perspective holds out the promise of a people bound together in mutual trust and compassion for one another.

The Moral Majority serves neither the justice, the dignity, nor the compassion which Jesus demands of his followers. The Christian Right has created a theology for the strong and powerful, and it serves their interests well although it does not claim to belong to them. But the only "true" theology from the Bible's point of view is theology which leads us to a proper relationship among people and therefore with God. Christians call that *justice*. The Moral Majority is neither familiar with nor interested in that goal, even though it is what its audiences need most of all.

A theology which seeks justice and affirms the dignity of every human being, as we promise at our baptism, does not enflame the division between the poor and the nearly poor; it calls us to respect and care for both. It calls Christians to work so that all human beings have the power to be what God wills them to be—free people. It strives to support institutions based on respect and mutual support—in the home, at work, in the school and the marketplace. It seeks to defuse and transcend power. It is diligent in making peace, not war, the highest goal. It helps the weak to power in the interest of our common humanity. It calls us all to a new kind of world.

Any true Christian theology is dedicated not to the past but the future. Any authentic Christian faith trusts God to lead us where we have not yet been, and welcomes the pilgrimage into the *not-yet*. We know that what God has in store for us remains to be seen, and the hints we have encountered from time to time make us eager to get on with the dream. For Christians, the past is pregnant with promise, but only with promise. We look backward only to move on. That is the posture of hope to which we are called.

The Moral Majority has no such theology. It has instead a bankrupt ideology which celebrates our divisions, feasts on powerlessness, and changes nothing. It fosters an image of the world which guarantees the continued victimization of its own supporters as well as those who are weaker still. It proclaims a false America, a distorted family, a lifeless church, a tyrant deity. In doing so, it fails America, its people, and its God.

# 8

# Meeting the Challenge

The Great Awakening which swept over the American colonies in the mid-eighteenth century began in the church but spread rapidly beyond its boundaries. Very soon, it had become a movement which called to people from outside the churches to come and join them. Those who remained in the churches of the mainstream—Puritans, Presbyterians, and Anglicans—faced a serious challenge. They could ignore the Awakening, pretending that it would disappear; but they knew they would only be deceiving themselves. They found themselves forced by circumstances to *respond* to it: to decide what they thought about it and whether its appeal made sense. If they were to take it seriously, they had to be clear about what the Awakening meant to them, why people found it so attractive, and how the churches would have to change because of it. They had to choose whether they could join with it as allies, or if, and why, the movement must be resisted. It is safe to say that after the Great Awakening, the mainstream churches of America were never quite the same again.

The Awakenings were the first American religious movements to challenge the historic churches from outside that mainstream. The Moral Majority is the most recent. The churches of our own day can no more pretend to ignore the Christians of the New Right than our ancestors could overlook the challenges of their times.

The Moral Majority addresses itself more directly to those

outside or on the fringes than those of us inside the mainstream churches; nevertheless, the nature of its appeal means that we are directly affected. In the first place, our churches include dissatisfied members who find the perspective of the Christian Right attractive and compelling. Furthermore, the Moral Majority claims to speak as the authentic voice of Christianity in our time. That in itself is a challenge to the churches. It means that if we consider ourselves Christian, we have to decide if, and when, the Moral Majority is speaking for us, and whether we wish to agree that their message is the churches' last word. If not, we must somehow disassociate ourselves from them. But if we do not want to abandon the public forum to them altogether, the churches must be prepared to speak clearly in our own name. We must be able to spell out with clarity how we believe the Christian Right falls short of the faith and tradition of the church. That has been the chief intention of this book. But if we are serious about the unity of the Body of Christ we preach, we must also somehow move beyond argument and confrontation to encounter and dialogue.

I suggest that any adequate response to the Christian Right by the churches of the mainstream would entail four distinct but related components. The first is *comprehension*. We must be absolutely certain about what the Moral Majority believes, and also the unspoken implications of its faith. We must ask ourselves what the world would look like if its theology actually came to dominate the American political and religious scene. But we also need to grasp the nature of its appeal: we must understand why the Moral Majority has succeeded in gaining the attention and support of so many Americans.

Second, Christians in the churches of the mainstream must *examine their own tradition critically in the light of the Christian Right's successes*. What problems or failures on our part can we discern which might contribute to the Moral Majority's appeal? If every Christian movement which addresses the churches from outside contains at least an implicit judgment upon them, what shortcomings in our own community of faith can the Christians of the New Right help us to see? What can they tell us about ourselves? Or, more to the point, how can we learn from them about the reformation *we* need if the churches are to be more faithful?

Third, we should commit ourselves to *clarify our position and correct our mistakes in the light of that judgment.* The churches of the mainstream could spell out more clearly where we stand on the issues raised by the Christian Right. At the very least, this would have the effect of heightening our own awareness about what we believe in some critical areas. Beyond that, insofar as the Moral Majority thrives on the churches' failures, it might move the Christian mainstream in directions that would reduce the alienation from which the Christian Right springs.

And finally, the churches have an obligation to *reach towards dialogue* with their brothers and sisters to their right. A complete response to the Moral Majority comprises identifying points of contact and conversation where, having heard a word of judgment, the churches might risk a word of illumination in return. Just as the Christian Right can call us to faithfulness, they need to hear the churches' perspectives. We ought to be seeking ways to clarify our stance for ourselves and communicate it to those whose faith might be changed by a less narrowly confined gospel.

## Understanding the Moral Majority

Like the charismatic movement with which it shares the position of gadfly on the churches' periphery, by its very existence the Moral Majority tells us something about its own adherents but also about the churches of the mainstream. The charismatic movement delivers a clear message that those attracted to it seek religious experience. They want *God,* not information *about* God. The form of the charismatic revival indicates that, by and large, they have not found that experience in the churches.

In the same way, the Christian Right is telling us that they want to *belong,* and they want *clear values* to live by. The shape of the Christian Right as political and religious movement demonstrates that substantial numbers of people feel themselves alienated at every level of life, and that they have not found a remedy or alternative to that alienation in the churches. Nor have they discovered among the mainstream churches sufficient guidance and direction in the formation of values that will make it possible for them to live in a pluralistic world.

The confusion between politics and religion which leads the Moral Majority to attempt to create a twentieth-century "Christian commonwealth" demonstrates that the primary form of alienation they suffer so acutely is social. The political and social institutions of America have somehow failed to provide them with an adequate sense of identity and participation. They are certain that the decisions that matter to them, whether involving their family, their work, their neighborhood, or their country, are made without any reference to them. They feel ignored, unnoticed, superfluous. Somehow, the complicated systems and institutions devised for what we call "input" have failed them. Elections offer them a choice of candidates uniform in their failure to speak to issues that matter to them. Other peoples' problems seem more important. When they visit their children's schools, they are strangers, awkward and uncertain. The news they read is about other people, not themselves.

Such alienation from the dominant society has been true for Christians in a great many times and places, beginning with the first Christians in a hostile Roman Empire, and repeated, for example, throughout the long history of survival by Orthodox Christians in the Muslim East. Yet they were never tempted to the forms of extremist faith and practice to which the Christian Right succumbs, because the church always offered them an alternative community in which they found both acceptance and identity. No matter if the dominant culture was out to destroy them; within the household of faith they knew who they were, and their place was secure. However short the society fell of bestowing meaningful power on its Christian citizens, the power that counted—the power to live in accordance with their sense of purpose—was communicated through the church and its community life. Their social identity was secondary to the knowledge that their *true* identity was made clear to them in baptism; their *true* citizenship was in the City of God. They did not expect to have the opportunity to act out their destiny in a hostile world, so they were not disappointed.

Things are different for the Moral Majority and its audience. In the first place, they have been led by two centuries of political rhetoric to believe that we *can* in fact find our identity and purpose within society because it is built on biblical principles. The Christian Right is composed of the natural heirs of our common ancestors who believed that it was possible to realize the City of God in time and history. The Moral Majority cannot believe that they were wrong, in spite of the evidence to the contrary; so they go on seeking a perfect Christian America, and suffering because they have not found it. But a blurred distinction between social and religious identity has always confused the position of Christians in society.

History shows that whenever Christians attempt to create a "Christian" culture, the distinction between church and state tends to disappear. The church loses its independent existence and its critical stance. Given his presuppositions, Falwell's confusion of piety and patriotism is really inevitable. It means that his church simply blesses, without comment, his vision of America. But the same kind of confusion also means that the mainstream churches have become part of the dominant culture and are nearly indistinguishable from it. In other words, the churches form part of the "power elite" which the New Right sees as its enemy. The Christian Right cannot find its purpose and identity in the churches of the mainstream because those churches are part of the problem. They see the same values, the same style, the same people in the pulpit and the pews that they see dominating every other avenue of their life. They are deeply and painfully alienated from churches which they consider simply an integral part of the world of which they are victims. They hear no word of hope which they can identify as clearly addressed to *their* anxieties and fears. Their sense of being ignored and excluded in the areas where decisions are made about their lives extends to and includes the churches.

This alienation is experienced primarily as lack of power. It is for that reason that the Christian Right is part of a larger movement which seeks power for itself. It conceives of its place in society as an adversary relationship, and contemporary history as a battleground between those who have, and those who lack, power. It is determined to achieve the power it wants and needs by tackling the dominant class which shapes our institutions and culture; but the only model it has for defining its own goals is the model which it has inherited from the past, an image of society based more on rhetoric and illusion than fact. What is significant, however, is not only its dream of re-creating an America out of the past from which this time they will not be excluded; it is also important to note the vehemence of the Right's campaigns and its determination, for the first time in many years, not simply to defend itself but to *win.* The New Right means to "take over" America and its institutions, and remake them to its liking. As Paul Weyrich put it, "We're radicals working to overturn the present structure in this country. . . . We're talking about Christianizing America." [1]

The battle which has been undertaken is being fought in the name of *values,* because the New Right believes that those in power have failed them most in this regard. Part of the price of being excluded from the consensus which dominates society and its culture is the inability to participate in its values. Because the Right is made up of isolated and alienated people, it lacks the social cohesion to identify and articulate its own authentic values. Instead, it proclaims its allegiance to a set of values which are the only ones it knows, even though they are in fact derived from an illusory past. Of course, the dominant culture in America, like every culture, has clearly held values; but they are not the values of the New Right. The Right, separated from that culture, sees only permissiveness. It fears that if the imaginary and rhetorical values of the past are abandoned, they will not be replaced at all. Rather, they will find themselves in a state of what the French sociologist Emile Durkheim called *anomie:* a terrifying condition in which people are immobilized in the absence of any norms to tell them what to do. The New Right seems genuinely to believe that if it does not hold on to the only values it knows—however uncertain and inappropriate they may be—there will be moral chaos. It sees only two alternatives: what it calls "traditional" absolutes, and "anything goes." It defines ethical choices in black-and-white, either-or situations: *either* a Victorian model of the family *or* utter promiscuity; *either* censorship *or* pornography on every newsstand.

What that fear can tell us about the churches is that we have failed to communicate clearly the way ethics can function positively in a pluralistic society. The mainstream churches have not shown how we can still hold values while granting others the possibility of disagreement. We have failed to demonstrate the difference between freedom and anarchy.

## Judgment from the Right

The prophet Isaiah once shocked his people by speaking in God's name and calling Assyria "the rod of my anger." [2] They were astonished that God's judgment might be delivered from *outside* the covenant-community.

Christians tend to be equally shocked when we are reminded that we can sometimes learn lessons we need to hear from people outside our churches. I have no doubt that the Christian Right has a word of judgment for the mainstream churches from which it feels itself excluded. No response would be complete without listening carefully to what that movement can tell us about ourselves and the quality of the churches' life.

The Moral Majority is surely a testimony to our failure to

honor our baptismal promise to respect the dignity of every human being.

In recent years, the mainstream churches have begun to notice the plight of the world's most victimized people in ways they had not undertaken before. Images of the most wretched—victims of war and famine—have been branded into our consciences. Most of us will carry with us until we die gruesome pictures of African and Vietnamese children in pain. Their misery has called forth some noteworthy gestures of ministry, most recently the resettlement of thousands of "boat people" undertaken with the churches' cooperation.

The beginning of concern for global suffering is in part the outcome of an earlier awakening by the churches to the devastating effects of segregation on American blacks. During a brief period in the 1960s, the mainstream churches, at least at the official level, made significant commitments to the movement for freedom which began in the black churches. Many believe that the Civil Rights Act of 1964, which guaranteed full human rights to blacks for the first time since Reconstruction, would never have been passed without the support of the churches.

But it must also be said that the gestures of support which the mainstream churches make, and have made, on behalf of human liberation have tended to be directed towards those at some distance from us, whose lives bear few points of contact with middle-class America. The churches have, for the most part, ignored the needs of working-class Americans, who suffer from a somewhat different form of powerlessness but whose pain is just as real. The concerns of labor, of small-property owners and the entrepreneurs of family businesses, have rarely been noted by the churches. Their ethical dilemmas have received scant attention from the theologians. The strength of the Moral Majority is a word of judgment to the Christian mainstream, reminding us that we have not affirmed our unity with those whose oppression is less noticeable. We have delivered a message: Their pain doesn't matter.

Such insensitivity is a sign of our own bondage to the culture, the institutions, and the people who are "in charge." The truth is, the churches of the mainstream desperately need a critical theology to help us understand ourselves. (We might recall that being critical means making judgments, not being negative. No doubt there are positive aspects of our situation that deserve our support as well as problems that need correcting.)

In the past, we have only rarely turned a questioning eye upon the values we proclaim in our congregational life. We permit society's judgments to determine status in the church; the same people are usually pillars of both. Our social witness is rarely directed at "unpopular" causes, especially when they might embarrass or inconvenience members of our own congregations. Our causes are almost always chosen for us by the concerns of the culture of which we are a part. Christians almost never *lead* movements, even when they are dedicated to values which belong to us. The churches "discovered" racism, not by observing their own grotesquely racist institutional life but by having it pointed out to them in the courts and the classroom. Students, secular humanists, and "fringe Christians" shamed us into opposing the war in Vietnam. Ten years ago, atheists and agnostics had far more sensitivity to the status of women—including their place in the churches—than most Christians. We need to ask ourselves why Christians have to be reminded of when to fight for their own values. No doubt there are other unnoticed areas which challenge us now to witness to justice— and we don't even see them, because we allow the culture around us to tell us what matters. Until Christians learn how to cast a critical eye at *our own* situation—at the society and environment we call home, and at the churches' relationship to it—we will continue to be enslaved by it. It is one thing to conform to the styles and customs of a people in order to live among them; it is another to adapt so completely to their priorities that no one can tell how Christians are different from anyone else. Only a church which can see itself as it really is, in a world as it really is, will ever be free. Only a church which is not captive to the culture of the mainstream can address and welcome the whole human family.

The Moral Majority's fascination with ethical absolutes points to another way in which the churches are judged. For all their commitment to some aspects of social ethics, the churches have not, for the most part, nurtured a strong personal commitment to Christian values by their numbers. Parents often look in vain for assistance from their church in helping children to acquire the tools for making responsible choices. We have espoused a situational morality without teaching people the values and the decision-making skills they need to face the dilemmas which challenge them. No wonder people confuse the affirmation of personal freedom and responsibility with permissiveness and *laissez-faire* morality. We have not, in many cases, commended the sense of personal integrity on which a truly free person's character depends. We have been more concerned with *clarifying* situations than with proclaiming the values by which we can deal with them. The churches are right to move beyond what has been called code morality; it reduces ethics to moral book-keeping and violates the New Testament. But we have not always emphasized the prerequisites for living with the responsibility of ethical and moral freedom.

This is only one of the ways in which we have failed to prepare ourselves for a genuinely pluralistic world. We have come to understand that Christian faith, and Christian values, are only one way of living in the world. We can all name people of undoubted virtue and compassion who decline to have any contact with the church or organized religion. Furthermore, the world has shrunk so that the other world religions are no longer exotic and quaint material for the *National Geographic*. In many regions of our country, we are in daily contact with Muslims, Hindus, and Buddhists. We are becoming uncomfortably aware that to them, *our* values and customs appear strange and foreign. The churches have prepared us very poorly indeed for coping with what might be called the conflict of values and the clash of faith which accompanies it. The fact of pluralism is a challenge which the churches of the mainstream have failed to meet.

Pluralism leads some Christians out of faith altogether because they find it impossible to preserve any sense of the uniqueness and appeal of their own Christianity. Indeed, they are hard put to define any reason for holding any values at all. If they continue to participate in the life of the church, they do so cynically and out of habit or esthetic reasons. The Moral Majority attracts those equally troubled by pluralism who choose the opposite route, preferring to shut out dialogue and withdrawing into a religious and cultural ghetto where they can continue to clutch at the old absolutes from the days when "everybody" was a Christian.

Another related failure which the success of the Christian Right calls to our attention is our inability or unwillingness to communicate a clear sense of the nature and authority of the Bible. We have been quite successful in training our members not to take the Bible literally; we have failed utterly to convey how it is to be taken instead. Episcopalians have simply ignored the Bible, and the level of scriptural illiteracy among us is embarrassing. Many could probably not give more than a cursory repetition of familiar stories from the life of Jesus, vaguely recalled from childhood and refreshed by the habit of reading from the Gospels at celebrations of the Eucharist. The Old Testament is generally conceived as a book of mystery, perhaps worth reading were it not so difficult. The New Testament is barely more familiar; we all know Paul, but more by hearsay than by familiarity with his writings.

The mainstream churches, and my own Episcopal Church in particular, no longer seem to consider it important that their members know the scriptures thoroughly, nor that they know what to make of them. What precisely *is* the authority of the Bible for Christians? How much of the Bible must we believe, and what are the standards for deciding? How can we tell when it is to be taken as history, or as legend, or as myth? We have tended to mystify the scriptures so that only highly trained biblical scholars can interpret them for us. This "counterreformation" (in that it reverses the gesture with which the Reformation began, making the Bible available to all) severs the present experience of Christians from their past and their tradition, causing us to lose sight of our identity as the ongoing community of faith. The formidable story of the People of God from its beginnings to the growth of the Christian Church is *our* story. But the mainstream churches have not made that fact clear, nor have they given us the means we need to find ourselves in the story. The Moral Majority's fundamentalist and selective reading of scripture sometimes approaches travesty; but most of us cannot tell why, or offer the challenge of a more faithful approach to the Bible as an alternative.

Still another judgment which we can hear from the Right is the churches' failure to clarify the relationship between Christian and "secular" learning. All creation is God's, and no knowledge can ever contradict God's truth. But we have failed to explore the consequences of that statement, and for most Christians in the churches of the mainstream, faith and learning are confused. We have tended to ignore the profound truth expressed in the biblical view of reality because we have accepted, rightly, the scientific explanation of the *how* of creation. The Christian Right, on the other hand, would rather jettison or ignore the realm of secular learning than give up the theology of the Book of Genesis.

Each of these elements of judgment which the Moral Majority holds up before us challenges the churches of the mainstream. They show us all too clearly the shortcomings of the life of our community and the weaknesses of the ways in which we proclaim our common faith. There are, no doubt, concrete steps which the mainstream churches could take which would form a legitimate response to the criticisms implicit in the successes of the Christian Right. Perhaps they would clarify the Moral Majority's own distortions and lessen their appeal; at any rate, they would make the church more faithful.

## Putting the Mainstream's House in Order

If the churches began to examine out loud their own stance with regard to the institutions and culture which dominate our society, and showed signs of ending their submission to them, perhaps alienated people would be less likely to dismiss the churches as part of the establishment. Such a declaration of independence would be painful and costly. Our identification with power and our more or less uncritical support of it has brought us many advantages. Our chaplains serve as officers in hallowing our war efforts, our clergy are not liable to military service, our churches pay no taxes, and we are treated with vestigial deference. We are awarded the mantle of propriety and respectability, and flattered into believing that those in power care what the churches think. Few public officials consider their installation complete, few legislatures or chambers of commerce begin their deliberations, without our "official" representative on hand to assure them that God approves of them. Until the churches learn to distance themselves from alliances which obligate us to power, powerless people will *know* they are not part of us.

Freeing ourselves from too-close identification with power might well create the possibility for new kinds of participation in the churches' life. Leadership, for example, is not the exclusive prerogative of the middle class, but our churches give few opportunities unless social and ecclesiastical credentials are equally assuring. If the churches ever took a seriously critical stance towards their own ideological allegiances, they would see how difficult it is for people without particular kinds of tastes, education, and social skills to survive in our churches. We need genuinely *open* congregations, not only in principle but in practice. We may well post a sign on the corner to assure passersby that The Episcopal Church Welcomes You, but a short visit tells them how conditional that welcome might be. A genuinely faithful attitude to the church's mission would lead us beyond slogans towards worship, congregational life, programs of education and nurture, and denominational institutions, restructured in the direction of true inclusiveness. In the meantime, the potential populists will always know that they are more welcome among the Christian Right than in the stately sanctuaries of the mainstream.

A church critically aware of itself would not have to depend upon its surroundings to set its priorities. A truly inclusive church would develop forms of social ministry which would address the needs of those at our side as well as those safely removed from us. We need to complement our global concerns by a witness to issues of justice and dignity on our own doorstep. Local churches, for example, could pay far more attention to the survival of our neighborhoods. After all, Christians presumably have some experience in nurturing community. We are natural advocates for the healing of our neighborhoods—whether defending them against the ravages of "progress" in the form of an expressway that benefits those who pass through and destroys a community, or by helping a close-knit, ingrown neighborhood to move towards a healthy diversity.

Mainstream churches should be wise as serpents in noticing issues of economic justice nearby. They need not stand quietly by as arbitrary decisions made at long distances wreak havoc on jobs and families. The example of Youngstown, Ohio, can point our way. When a steel plant closed in that city and threw its economy into chaos, an ecumenical coalition took on the job of fighting on the side of the thousands left unemployed. The coalition's failure to achieve its goals should not blind us to the example: mainstream churches taking on the real-life issues that matter to people where they are. That kind of mission testifies to alienated people that they *do* matter.

Another area where the churches have an opportunity to put their collective wisdom to work in overcoming the divisions among us is by a positive, and critical, concern for the well-being of the family. Perhaps in part they are in bondage to the crass individualism and other cultural attitudes that disrupt families. But whatever the reasons, the mainstream churches have not spoken a critical word to a culture which has little use for marriage except as an arrangement of convenience.

It is time for the churches to affirm the value of marriage as a well-tested arena in which people can learn how to love each other. Founded on mutual commitment, it teaches us the meaning of caring for another person, the love and respect which God has shown us. The Episcopal Church's *Book of Common Prayer* suggests that people who have learned to love and be loved in marriage can turn outward to a needy world; their marriage strengthens and molds them into the compassionate and responsible people God wills them to be. It is time for the churches to say so loudly and clearly.

It is also time for us to distance ourselves from life-styles which affirm that the only value of sexuality is its ability to give pleasure. Christians take the flesh too seriously to degrade it in this way. Sexuality calls for the same commitment, responsibility, and respect for another human being that any truly human relationship demands. It is time for the mainstream churches to preach a *Christian* theology of sex, based on the goodness and promise of the flesh and the challenge to achieve a sexual relationship based on justice and dignity.

At the same time, our commitment to those values calls us to hold up a model of sexual behavior which puts those values into practice. It is time for the churches to proclaim that the value of marriage lies in the quality of life it creates. Many marriages exist in name only, rendered lifeless by violence which, even if directed towards one by the other, degrades both. Perhaps the Moral Majority would be able to see the need for marriage to be based on more humane values if the churches of the mainstream were more able to recall that marriage can be a sign of God's own promises.

There is more to morality than the narrow sexual focus of the Christian Right. Clear teaching about the possibility for living our Christian values in the context of a family could be augmented by a firmer commitment on the part of the churches to commend its own values. We tend to act as if they were simply part of the culture, but they are not. Rather, they offer the possibility of a life enhanced and made more fully human than the culture dreams. Christians have inherited from our spiritual ancestors the values on which the City of God is built, and it is time for us to say so clearly. The requirement for justice among Christians is not fulfilled by being honest with your tax return; there is more to it than that. Love goes beyond charity and the United Way. Peace is not a restful feeling; it is the condition, and the definition, of human well-being. Dignity is not an optional possibility; where it is absent, the human family experiences indescribable suffering. Justice is not a goal for idealists, but the requirement for living as fully human beings. Christians sometimes seem to forget how necessary these biblical values are to the practice of faith. The scriptures assure us that they are required for faithfulness. Values shape the way Christians live in the world, and eventually can become so much a part of us that they form our character. But that is the end of a long journey of faith and commitment. It is time for the churches of the mainstream to remind ourselves, so that we can remind others, of the opportunity to become a people whose values reflect the values of Christ. That is part of the promise of being human.

Perhaps we would be more aware of those values if the mainstream churches emphasized a genuinely critical study of the Bible. We need the scholarly tools for getting at what the biblical writers meant and understanding the world that shaped their concerns. It is crucial for us to know as much as we can about the events and biases of their lives. But critical reading of their story also means discovering how it judges *us*. We need to become familiar with how our own needs and fears and hopes were present among the people of the Bible, and how their adventures with God and the world light up our own. The authority of the Bible comes not from details of history or world view, which might well be senseless to us; its authority comes from being the means by which we find God in our past. Its authority is the authority the past can always have for us: it gives us identity and direction, and calls us to add our own experience to the legacy of the generations. We are creating the story of the People of God; our experience of faith will become part of that tradition. Our life of faith makes sense only in the context of what has gone before.

Although our churches have contact with people in positions of secular learning and wisdom, they sometimes act as if we have nothing to say to each other except on what we consider "common ground"—the tiny pieces of life where faith and reason overlap. We step back from the wonders of modern physics, biology, genetics, and astronomy, and hope only that by their presence in our pews the practitioners of such wonders will testify to us that, yes, it is still possible to be religious in the twentieth century. We are so relieved that we fail to ask what sleight of mind they perform in order to move between the two realms, science and religion.

The churches ought instead to be exploring with sympathetic scientists and scholars the ways in which their discoveries touch the life of faith. Faith requires a world view, and science helps mold that view. The infinity of space gives us a very different conception of God, and our place in the universe, than the ceilinged and earth-centered universe of the Middle Ages. We *need* science to help us build the world view within which we seek to be faithful. But the scientists need the churches to challenge them to explain themselves: What are the implications for the human race of their discoveries? Christians have every right to ask what is the *point* of scientific discovery and experiment, because it is too dangerous if we do not. There is no value-free learning. It will benefit someone, and we must ask whom. To raise these questions is not to disparge the search for truth and understanding, but to issue a warning about how it is to be used. There is no ultimate contradiction between faith and reason. If the churches were more attentive to the bonds between them, people would not feel the need to choose one or the other.

Finally, the Moral Majority ҫhallenges the churches to be clear about what we belive about *power*. The Christian Right believes that God is best defined in terms of power, and it makes that claim on the basis of its experience of life in the world—and in the church. A faithful Christian community has to show, both by its teaching and by its own life, that there is another alternative than power for understanding God—and God's image, the human family. The Moral Majority is right that we all need power; but it is not power to dominate others but power to take charge of our own destiny. That is the power God wills for us in creation, and shows us in baptism because we are the children of God. It is power to be who we can become. Christian faith tells us that such power comes to fulfillment when we give others the same power to be themselves. This mutual respect is the basis of life as the church is meant to practice it. It is the greatest challenge of this and every age: to be people of justice, which means claiming God's promise for ourselves, the power to be, and granting the same promise to others—the power to let them be. When we live in such a way, we reflect the very nature of God.

## Addressing the Christian Right

If the churches of the mainstream heeded the challenge of the Moral Majority, they might look and speak in such a way that the Christian Right would be willing to listen. But our own perspective gives us a challenge to them as well. We have a message for the Christian Right which might serve as meeting point for informal encounter.

However, if there is to be meaningful conversation between the mainstream religious community and the New Right, it must take place in an atmosphere of respect which affirms the diginity of those who side with the Moral Majority. There is no place for smugness or superiority in our dialogue.

The mainstream churches ought to challenge the Moral Majority to be more honest about history. Their image of the America of the past is so distorted as to be only a shadow of the whole truth about us. Part of the problem, of course, is that the Christian Right is not incarnate in institutions which have continuity. But the churches do have traditions. They have a past which extends back into the early years of America, and they know about that past. The churches need to speak forthrightly to the radical Right to tell them that their vision of America is false.

It is false because it defines the American dream too narrowly. The dream was formed not only by Puritans and the heirs of the Great Awakening, but by Deists who denied the divinity of Christ, by intellectuals who considered all religious dogma to be superstitious, by Jewish and Roman Catholic immigrants who fed the dream by following it at great cost, by Africans brought against their will but who still caught the promise of freedom, and by aliens even today who risk swimming the Rio Grande or spend days in tiny boats because they have heard that there is hope here. To try to confine the American dream to its most narrow form distorts and violates it. The dream meant that a society in which mutual well-being was possible could be built by people who held radically different values and preconceptions. By defining the dream to meet their own wishes and fantasies, the Christian Right destroys it. We must continue to explain why, and how, that is so.

The mainstream churches have no right to fault the Christian Right for its involvement in politics; the churches have always been identified, and rightly, with the nature and quality of our life together. But we need to differentiate between affirming values that matter to us, and insisting that only one course, or candidate, is possible for Christians. We must remember that

Christians who agree about values may well disagree about how they can best be realized in a specific situation. The Bible sets priorities and leaves us free to decide how best to act upon them.

The Christian Right's single-mindedness flies in the face of the democratic pluralism on which America is built; we must show why this is true. It also contradicts the principle of individual responsibility on which Christian ethics depends; we must explain why this is so. The Bible warns us that discerning God's will is often risky and difficult. We must demonstrate the defensive arrogance of calling oneself and one's allies a "moral majority." As People for the American Way, a group organized to encourage tolerance and diversity, observed: "We are not opposing the Religious New Right for speaking out on political matters—all people have the right and responsibility to state their beliefs. We are concerned, however, about an extraordinary attempt to impose a rigid interpretation on what is and is not a 'Christian' response to our troubled times. We want a national climate that encourages and enhances the human spirit—not one that divides human beings into opposing and hostile camps."[3]

I believe that the Christian Right might also be challenged by the churches with regard to its use of the scriptures. There are Christians whose respect for the Bible is as absolute, and whose interpretation is every bit as conservative, as that of the Moral Majority, but who do not stop at the proof text but examine the biblical witness as a whole. Such Christians achieve a radical commitment to justice and dignity. The Christian Right should be challenged to such a complete vision of the Bible.

Then the Moral Majority might be able to see the points at which the biblical perspective judges America—not on the special, narrowly conceived issues so dear to its heart but on the much more basic biblical issues of justice and human dignity. It if did so, then the New Right might arrive at a more critical attitude towards America as the Promised Land. That ideological doctrine does nothing for Christian faith, and pushes patriotism into idolatry. A religious viewpoint which is genuinely biblical should be able to see that. The City of God is the promise at the end of history, towards which we still strive. As God's destiny for us all, it provides us with a criterion for judging every time and every nation. Giving up its ideology of America would move the Moral Majority towards a more authentic biblical commitment to building the signs of the humanity to which we are called.

\*     \*     \*     \*     \*

As we always have been, we Americans are a nation divided between those who belong and those outside clamoring to be let in. That division, which has warped our society since its beginning, survives in forms which change and yet remain remarkably the same. The spirit and passion and rage of William Jennings Bryan live on in the Falwells of our time. They are no nearer than their forebears to achieving what they want—or what they need. And we must ask if our churches are any more prepared than they were in the past to open themselves to all our people. The gulf is ancient and broad. We need bridges; we need signs of hope and encounter.

Most of all, perhaps, we need a new kind of society where no one is left out, and a new kind of church which mirrors in its life the hope for the whole human family.

That is a goal worthy of all who call themselves Christians.

# Notes

*Chapter 1*

1. Jerry Falwell, *Listen, America!* (Garden City: Doubleday, 1980), p. 266.
2. Paul Weyrich, director of the Committee for the Survival of a Free Congress, quoted in Thomas J. McIntyre, *The Fear Brokers* (Boston: Beacon Press, 1979), p. 67.
3. Falwell, *Listen, America!* p. 252.
4. Ibid., pp. 21–22.
5. Ibid., p. 29.
6. Ibid.
7. Ibid., p. 63.
8. Ibid., p. 69.
9. Ibid., p. 98.
10. Ibid., p. 69.
11. Ibid., p. 74.
12. Quoted in ibid., pp. 70–71.
13. Ibid., p. 74.
14. Ibid., pp. 128–29.
15. Ibid., p. 129.
16. Cal Thomas, "Another View," *Moral Majority Report* 2 (22 June 1981): 4.
17. Falwell, *Listen, America!* p. 179.
18. Ibid., p. 87.
19. Ibid., p. 106.
20. Ibid., p. 95.
21. Ibid., p. 98.
22. Ibid., pp. 207–8.

23. George McDearmon, "The Christian and Politics," *Christian Times,* December 1980, p. 11.

24. Mike Feinsilber, "Three Congressmen Quit Pro-Life Group," *Wilmington* (Del.) *Evening Journal,* 4 June 1981.

25. Adam Clymer, "For Moral Majority: A Step toward '82," *New York Times,* 14 June 1981.

26. Falwell, *Listen, America!* pp. 258–59.

27. Peter Marshall and David Manuel, *The Light and the Glory* (Old Tappan, N.J.: Revell, 1977), pp. 355, 359.

28. Joe Klein, "The Moral Majority's Man in New York," *New York Magazine,* 18 May 1981, p. 26.

29. William Martin, "The Birth of a Media Myth," *The Atlantic* 247 (June 1981): 7, 10–16; James L. Franklin, "The Religious Right: Its Political Clout Appears Overstated," *Boston Globe,* 19 July 1981.

30. Alan Crawford, *Thunder on the Right: The 'New Right' and the Politics of Resentment* (New York: Pantheon, 1980), pp. 48–49.

31. Frances FitzGerald, "A Reporter at Large: A Disciplined, Charging Army," *The New Yorker,* 18 May 1981, p. 89.

32. Television broadcasts, June 1981.

33. Television broadcast, June 1981.

34. Crawford, *Thunder on the Right,* pp. 10–13.

35. Clymer, "For Moral Majority," p. 36.

36. Quoted in Crawford, *Thunder on the Right,* p. 183.

37. Quoted in Klein, "Moral Majority's Man," p. 28.

38. Falwell, *Listen, America!* p. 179.

39. Ibid., pp. 255–56.

*Chapter 2*

1. S. E. Morison, "Puritans and the Life of the Mind," in David D. Hall, ed., *Puritanism in Seventeenth Century Massachusetts* (New York: Holt, Rinehart & Winston, 1968), p. 16.

2. John Winthrop, "A Model of Christian Charity," in Conrad Cherry, ed., *God's New Israel: Religious Interpretations of American Destiny* (Englewood Cliffs, N.J.: Prentice-Hall, 1971), p. 43.

3. Peter Marshall and David Manuel, *The Light and the Glory* (Old Tappan, N.J.: Revell, 1977), p. 210.

4. Ibid., p. 212.

5. Ibid., p. 25.

6. Robert N. Bellah, "Civil Religion in America," in Rusell E. Richey and Donald G. Jones, eds., *American Civil Religion* (New York: Harper & Row, 1974).

7. Ibid., p. 25.

8. Ezra Stiles, "The United States Elevated to Glory and Honour," in Cherry, *God's New Israel,* p. 88.

9. John 3:1–21.

10. Robert T. Handy, *A Christian America* (New York: Oxford University Press, 1971), p. 29.

11. Richard Hofstadter, *Anti-Intellectualism in American Life* (New York: Random House, 1962), p. 80.

12. Alexis de Tocqueville, *Democracy in America* (New York: The Colonial Press, 1899), 1: 409.

13. Ibid., 1: 420.

14. Marvin Meyers, "The Restoration of the Old Republic Theme in the Jacksonian Persuasion," in James L. Bugg, ed., *Jacksonian Democracy, Myth or Reality?* (New York: Holt, Rinehart & Winston, 1962), p. 112.

15. Ibid., pp. 114–15.

16. Richard Hofstadter, *The Paranoid Style in American Politics and Other Essays* (Chicago: University of Chicago Press, 1979), p. 52.

17. George McKenna, "Populism: The American Ideology," *American Populism* (New York: Putnam, 1974), p. xii.

18. Hofstadter, *Anti-Intellectualism,* p. 108.

19. Hofstadter, *Paranoid Style,* p. 270.

20. McKenna, "Populism," p. xvi.

21. Hofstadter, *Anti-Intellectualism,* p. 121.

22. Ibid., p. 127.

23. Quoted in ibid., p. 125.

24. Quoted in ibid., pp. 126–27.

25. Quoted in ibid., p. 127.

26. Hofstadter, *Paranoid Style,* p. 87.

27. Quoted in Hofstadter, *Anti-Intellectualism,* pp. 124–25.

28. McKenna, "Populism," p. 213.

29. Quoted in ibid., pp. 214–15.

30. Quoted in Daniel Bell, *The Radical Right* (Garden City: Doubleday, 1963), pp. 15–16.

31. Quoted in McKenna, "Populism," p. 223.

32. Quoted in ibid., p. 229.

33. Quoted in Alan Crawford, *Thunder on the Right: The 'New Right' and the Politics of Resentment* (New York: Pantheon, 1980), p. 306.

34. Richard A. Viguerie, *The New Right: We're Ready to Lead* (Falls Church, Va.: The Viguerie Company, 1981), p. 8.
35. "Introduction by Jerry Falwell," ibid., unnumbered.
36. Ibid., p. 8.
37. Ibid., p. 9.
38. Ibid., p. 15.
39. Ibid., p. 16.
40. Ibid., p. 187.
41. "Introduction by Jerry Falwell," ibid., unnumbered.

*Chapter 3*

1. Quoted in Alan Crawford, *Thunder on the Right: The 'New Right' and the Politics of Resentment* (New York: Pantheon, 1980), p. 159.
2. Peter Marshall and David Manuel, *The Light and the Glory* (Old Tappan, N.J.: Revell, 1977), p. 25.
3. Jerry Falwell, *Listen, America!* (Garden City: Doubleday, 1980), p. 246.
4. Ibid., p. 64.
5. Quoted in Frances FitzGerald, "A Reporter at Large: A Disciplined, Charging Army," *The New Yorker,* 18 May 1981, p. 63.
6. Ibid., p. 64.
7. Kenneth Cauthen, "The Legitimacy and Limits of Freedom of Choice," *Christian Century* XCVIII (1981): 702.
8. Richard Hofstadter, *The Paranoid Style in American Politics and Other Essays* (Chicago: University of Chicago Press, 1979), p. 58.
9. Ibid., p. 51.
10. Quoted in Peter Steinfels, *The Neo-Conservatives: The Men Who Are Changing America's Politics* (New York: Simon & Schuster, 1980), pp. 38–39.
11. I Corinthians 1:18–25.
12. Matthew 25:40.
13. Martin E. Marty, *The Public Church: Mainline—Evangelical— Catholic* (New York: Crossroad Publishing Company, 1981), p. 138.
14. 1 John 4:19.
15. Isaiah 1:11–17.
16. Micah 6:8.

17. *Does the Bible Predict the Future?* (Virginia Beach: Christian Broadcasting Network, 1980).
18. Hal Lindsey *The 1980s: Countdown to Armageddon* (New York: Bantam, 1981), p. 12.
19. *Pat Robertson's Perspective,* March 1981.

*Chapter 4*

1. Jerry Falwell, *Listen, America!* (Garden City: Doubleday, 1980), p. 100.
2. Ibid., p. 98.
3. Ibid., p. 99.
4. Ibid., p. 98.
5. New York: Holt, Rinehart & Winston, 1981.
6. Washington: Ethics and Public Policy Center, 1979.
7. William E. Simon, *A Time for Truth* (New York: Berkley, 1978), p. 5.
8. Ibid., pp. 46–47.
9. Ibid., p. 47.
10. Ibid., p. 27.
11. Ibid., p. 26.
12. Falwell, *Listen, America!* p. 13.
13. Ibid., p. 148.
14. Ibid., p. 170.
15. Ibid., p. 171.
16. Letter from Faye Wattleton, Planned Parenthood of America, 1981.
17. Bob Schmidt, "Fundamentalist Parents Take Evolution to Court," *San Jose* (Calif.) *Mercury-News,* 1 March 1981.
18. "Judge Backs Teaching of Evolution to 'Creationist'," *New York Times,* 14 June 1981.
19. "Louisiana to Teach 'Creation'," *New York Times,* 22 July 1981.
20. *TV Guide,* 13–19 June 1981, p. A-105.
21. Isaac Asimov, "The 'Threat' of Creationism," *New York Times Magazine,* 14 June 1981, p. 100.
22. Ibid., 101.
23. Falwell, *Listen, America!* p. 205.
24. Ibid., p. 210.
25. Quoted in ibid., pp. 211–12.

26. Dena Kleiman, "Influential Couple Scrutinize Books for 'Anti-Americanism'," *New York Times,* 14 July 1981.

27. "Report on Book Censorship in Public Schools," National Coalition Against Censorship, New York, March 1981.

28. Richard A. Viguerie, *The New Right: We're Ready to Lead* (Falls Church, Va.: The Viguerie Company, 1981), pp. 133–34.

29. Quoted in "New SST: Threat to Freedom?" *The Witness* 64 (June 1981): 3, 17.

30. Richard Hofstadter, *The Paranoid Style in American Politics and Other Essays* (Chicago: University of Chicago Press, 1979), p. 63. In a 1965 essay, Hofstadter cautioned that his thesis should not be taken to mean that social mobility in the United States has been decreasing. See "Pseudo-Conservatism Revisited," in *Paranoid Style,* pp. 66–92.

31. Quoted in Nat Hentoff, "The Supreme Court's a Long Way from Poor Valley," *Village Voice,* 4–10 March 1981.

32. Letter from Norman Dorsen, American Civil Liberties Union, New York, 1981.

33. Viguerie, *New Right,* p. 107.

34. Luke 12:16–21.

35. Matthew 19:23–26.

36. Matthew 22:21.

37. "Primates Explore Poverty, Authority, Disarmament," Press Release, Diocesan Press Service, 7 May 1981, Appendix C, "Christian Attitudes to War in a Nuclear Age," p. 7.

38. George F. Regas, *Reversing the Arms Race: The Quintessential Task of the Church* (Cincinnati: Forward Movement, 1981), p. 9.

39. "Reagan Plans Flawed, NCCC Says," *NCCC Chronicles* 81 (Summer 1981): 6.

40. Quoted in Viguerie, *New Right,* p. 66.

41. Quoted in Donald E. Messer, "Panama Canal Treaties: Answering Questions on Main Street America," *Christian Century* XCV (1978): 17.

42. Thomas J. McIntyre, *The Fear Brokers* (Boston: Beacon Press, 1979), p. 128. Italics mine.

43. Falwell, *Listen, America!* p. 107.

44. Ibid., p. 113.

45. Mark Hatfield, *Between a Rock and a Hard Place* (Waco, Texas: Word Books, 1976), p. 38.

46. Ibid., p. 27.

*Chapter 5*

1. Quoted in *Moral Majority Report* 2 (20 July 1981): 2.
2. Jerry Falwell, *Listen, America!* (Garden City: Doubleday, 1980), p. 150.
3. Carolyn G. Heilbrun, *Reinventing Womanhood* (New York: Norton, 1979), p. 189.
4. Falwell, *Listen, America!* p. 121.
5. Ibid., p. 121.
6. Ibid.
7. 1 Peter 3:7.
8. Falwell, *Listen, America!* p. 151.
9. Ibid., p. 150.
10. Ibid., p. 183.
11. Quoted in ibid., pp. 129–30.
12. Ibid., p. 150.
13. Ibid., p. 124.
14. Ibid., p. 150.
15. Ibid.
16. Ibid., p. 151.
17. Ibid., p. 183.
18. Ibid., p. 182.
19. Ibid.
20. Ibid., p. 186.
21. Orrin Hatch and Jeremiah Denton, Letter to the Editor, *New York Times,* 15 June 1981.
22. Brochure, *"Let Their Eyes Be Opened": A Documentary about Humanism and Its Influences in the Schools. Humanism,* Virginia Beach, Virginia.
23. Bette Norman, "What's the Matter with Public Schools," *Christian Courier* 3 (September 1980): 1.
24. Ibid., p. 2.
25. Brochure: *Better Than Ever: The Bible Story* (San Jose, Calif.: Home Health Education Service, n.d.).
26. Deryl Edwards, "Jepsen, Laxalt, Smith Say Americans Want to Strengthen Family," *Moral Majority Report* 2 (20 July 1981): 10; *The Family Protection Act, 97th Congress, Concept Summary* (Office of Roger W. Jepsen, United States Senate).
27. Cal Thomas, "California Tries for Traditional Values," *Moral Majority Report* 2 (20 July 1981): 1.

28. *"Women Have Always Worked: A Historical Overview* by Alice Kessler-Harris," reviewed by Olive P. Hackett. *Radical Religion* 5 (n.d.): 28.
29. Ibid., p. 31.
30. Quoted in ibid., pp. 29–30.
31. Richard A. Viguerie, *The New Right: We're Ready to Lead* (Falls Church, Va.: The Viguerie Company, 1981), p. 28.
32. Ibid., p. 33.
33. Ibid., p. 103.
34. Quoted in Heilbrun, *Reinvesting Womanhood,* p. 175.
35. Ibid.
36. Ibid., p. 189.
37. Ibid., p. 196.
38. Ibid., p. 189.
39. Ibid., p. 196.
40. Ephesians 5:22–25, 6:1–4.
41. 1 Peter 3:1–7.
42. 1 Timothy 5:9–16
43. Mark 3:34.
44. Matthew 10:34.
45. Luke 9:59–60.
46. 1 Corinthians 7:9.
47. Galatians 3:28.
48. Walter Wink, "Biblical Perspectives on Homosexuality," *Christian Century,* XCVI (1979): 1085.
49. William Barnwell, "The Gays and the Divorced: Similar Scars," *Christian Century,* XCV (1978): 17.
50. John Boswell, *Christianity, Social Tolerance and Homosexuality: Gay People in Western Europe from the Beginning of the Christian Era to the Fourteenth Century* (Chicago and London: University of Chicago Press, 1980), p. 334.
51. Ibid., p. 295.
52. Falwell, *Listen, America!* p. 285.

*Chapter 6*

1. Letter, Pat Robertson, "700 Club," Virginia Beach, Virginia, n.d.
2. Mark R. Sills, "The Docetic Church," *Christian Century,* XCVIII (1981): 37.
3. Letter, Pat Robertson, Virginia Beach, Va.
4. "700 Club New Member Response Card."

5. Quoted in William F. Fore, "Beyond the Electronic Church," *Christian Century,* XCVIII (1981): 29.
6. William F. Fore, "The Electronic Church," *Ministry* 52 (January 1979): 6.
7. Ibid.
8. The United Presbyterian Foundation, New York.
9. Dr. Everett Koop, quoted in Robert Schuller, *How to Live Confidently in Troubled Times* (Garden Grove, Calif.: Hour of Power, 1980), p. 29.
10. Cavett Robert, quoted in ibid., p. 66.
11. Warren Duffy, quoted in ibid., pp. 47–49.
12. Dr. Joseph Jacobs, quoted in ibid., p. 80.
13. Order Form: Books and Cassette Albums by Robert Schuller.
14. Letter, Pat Robertson, "700 Club," Virginia Beach, Va.
15. Sills, "Docetic Church," pp. 37–38.
16. Fore, "Electronic Church," p. 5.
17. Fore, "Beyond the Electronic Church," p. 30.
18. Ibid.
19. Schuller, *How to Live,* p. 3.
20. Galatians 5:1.
21. Peter Berger, "The Class Struggle in American Religion," *Christian Century,* XCVIII (1981): 194.
22. Ibid., p. 197.
23. Luke 6:26.

*Chapter 7*

1. James 1:27.
2. See, e.g., Matthew 25:31–46.
3. Quoted in Charles Austin, "Brooklyn Pastor Assails Moral Majority's Leader," *New York Times,* 1 August 1981.

*Chapter 8*

1. Paul Weyrich, quoted in *Are We All God's People?* (Washington, D.C.: People for the American Way, n.d.).
2. Isaiah 10:5.
3. *Are We All God's People?*